Nambride de Nigri

Heaven to All Who Love

Nambride de Nigri

Heaven to All Who Love

ISBN/EAN: 9783744659949

Printed in Europe, USA, Canada, Australia, Japan

Cover: Foto ©Thomas Meinert / pixelio.de

More available books at **www.hansebooks.com**

HEAVEN TO ALL WHO LOVE.

BY THE
ABBÉ NAMBRIDE DE NIGRI.

𝔗𝔯𝔞𝔫𝔰𝔩𝔞𝔱𝔢𝔡 from the 𝔉𝔯𝔢𝔫𝔠𝔥
BY
MADAME R. A. VAIN.

"We know that we have passed from death to life, because we have loved the brethren.
"He that loveth not, abideth in death."—I. St. John, iii. 14.

LONDON:
THOMAS RICHARDSON AND SON;
26, PATERNOSTER ROW;
9, CAPEL STREET, DUBLIN; AND DERBY.
MDCCCLXXIV.

APPRECIATION

OF

MONSEIGNEUR BAGNOUX,

BISHOP OF BETHLEHEM,

REGARDING THE WORKS OF THE

ABBÉ NAMBRIDE DE NIGRI.

TO THE ABBÉ NAMBRIDE DE NIGRI.

Reverend Sir,

I received with indescribable pleasure your two splendid books, and perused them with all that attention they merited. I congratulate you for having composed these excellent works, and I thank the Almighty for having thus inspired you.

In the first of these works, "Heaven to all who Love," you expound the sense of the Divine Scriptures with a rare perfection. The first colloquies elevate the soul to God, and the succeeding ones fill the heart with indulgence for our fellow men, and form, at the same time, an admirable treatise on the Divine mercy. Your words are calculated to bring effectual consolation to feeble, disquieted, and timorous souls. The spirit the most depressed at the contemplation of its failings, will not peruse these eloquent pages without being restored to sentiments of confidence, and thereby incited to that true repentance which leads to sanctification.

Your second work, " Solace to all who Suffer," is, for all understandings, a splendid ray of light. You resolve the mystery of hereditary suffering through another mystery, namely, that of the Sacred Trinity; a sublime exposition, which confutes all the objections of the incredulous philosophers.

Spirits subdued by sophisms will not read those pages without being confounded, and several,—as I should venture to hope,—will thank you from their hearts.

In a word, your second book affords to all who mourn, and to all sorrowing hearts, the most rational balm, and the sweetest of consolations.

You have perfectly comprehended the human heart; return thanks to the Almighty, for having inspired you to express, in so sublime a style, those profound thoughts which are most fitting to console it.

Accept, Reverend Abbé, my sincere acknowledgments for your precious gifts, together with the assurance of my high esteem.

Yours most sincerely,

✠ STEPHEN, Bishop of Bethlehem,
Abbot of St. Maurice.

PREFACE.

What is the object meant to be attained by the present work? It is to exemplify the frightful division which exists amongst souls, to show forth the cause of that division, and to point out a remedy.

There are few men who love, and there are several others who do not love as they should love; and this is the source of that division that strikes our regard.

To elevate the heart to God, that it may devote itself to the souls of men, to destroy within ourselves all that which can separate us from our fellow men, to unite with them by exterior acts—herein lies the remedy.

To whom is this book addressed? To all; inasmuch as all men should mutually aid and unite with each other.

O you who seek to understand the depth of this word: "love one another;" do you open and read.

CONTENTS.

FIRST COLLOQUY.

The Disciple contemplates the harmonies of nature, and falls into sadness in seeing how souls live in dispersion and isolation—He demands of the Master by what means he may endeavour to establish harmony amongst them—The Master replies that before undertaking this task he must needs elevate himself to the love of heavenly things,   1

SECOND COLLOQUY.

The Disciple demands by what means he may arrive at the love of heavenly things, at sacrifice and union—The Master replies that he must pray—The Disciple complains: he has prayed according to his own will, and without uniting himself to the will of his Master—The Master instructs him in what manner he should pray,   73

THIRD COLLOQUY.

The Disciple demands in what manner it is fitting to love souls and labour for the establishment of harmony amongst them—The Master replies that before all things it is needful to prepare the heart—He teaches him not to judge, because judgment destroys love—He teaches him not to speak against his brethren, because the malicious word severs brother from brother, ... 97

FOURTH COLLOQUY.

The Master instructs His Disciple how to unite with his brothers by exterior acts—He teaches him how he should listen to those who need consolation, and how he should speak to them—The Master likewise teaches the Disciple how to solace the disinherited of the goods of this earth, so as to prepare the hearts of all who suffer, to listen to the words of life, ... 133

FIFTH COLLOQUY.

The Disciple demands to bear to souls the word of life—The Master replies to him that the hour is come when he may speak—He instructs him how to guard his heart in patience—He counsels him not to break the bruised reed, or to extinguish the smoking torch—The Master teaches all these things by His example, ... 161

SIXTH COLLOQUY.

The Disciple has done as the Master had counselled him, but the people of souls has not listened to him, and he is sad—The Master replies to him, that till this moment he has had within his heart no love save that which receives, but that the hour is come when He shall teach him a new love.

This love is that which pursues, and which seeks.

The Disciple demands of the Master by what means he may bring back the soul which has gone astray, in the ways of evil.

The Master instructs him how to speak, showing him what shall be the power of his words.

The Master teaches all these things by His example, 207

SEVENTH COLLOQUY.

The Disciple has spoken with the souls, and they have hearkened to his voice; yet, notwithstanding, sorrow re-enters his heart—He has beheld these souls take a holy flight towards the pure and celestial spheres, and now, he has ceased to see them—He demands of the Master if there be in the fire of love some germ, potent and fertile, that may raise that which was fallen and revive that which is dead—The Master replies; he who loves, pardons, and pardon upraises souls; He recommends His disciple to pardon seventy times seven times.

The Master teaches all these things by His example, 235

The Vision, ... 285

FIRST COLLOQUY.

THE DISCIPLE CONTEMPLATES THE HARMONIES OF NATURE, AND FALLS INTO SADNESS IN SEEING HOW SOULS LIVE IN DISPERSION AND ISOLATION.—HE DEMANDS OF THE MASTER BY WHAT MEANS HE MAY ENDEAVOUR TO ESTABLISH HARMONY AMONGST THEM. — THE MASTER REPLIES THAT BEFORE UNDERTAKING THIS TASK HE MUST NEEDS ELEVATE HIMSELF TO THE LOVE OF HEAVENLY THINGS.

FIRST COLLOQUY.

I.

I saw the sun as he rose above the horizon chasing away the shadows of the forests.

I saw the earth harmonise with the glories of the heavens, and present to my eyes the riches of her vegetation, with the magnificence of her fields and the brightness of her waters.

I inhaled the enchanting odour of her perfumed plants.

I heard the charming melody of the birds, that she nourishes in giving to each one its fitting pasture.

And, in presence of this loveliness I exclaimed; "Lord, Lord, Thou art grand in Thy works, and infinite is Thy power!"

The last words of this hymn of thankfulness and of love were still resounding, when, lo! my soul was suddenly wrapped in profound sadness.

O, my divine Master! Thou who knowest all things, Thou dost know wherefore I am sad.

Thou knowest why the splendours of nature

have greeted mine eyes without bringing to my heart peace or true joy.

Thou knowest that my soul, inspired with enthusiasm in the presence of the harmonies of this visible universe, has sought for other harmonies—but that seeking for them in vain, her song of joyfulness has been hushed, and sadness has come over her.

She is sad, because this people of souls that Thou hast created does not move in the same order as does this world of spheres that Thou hast launched into immensity.

She is sad, because that whilst sphere illumines sphere, so many souls will not enlighten their kindred souls.

She is sad, because whilst sphere tends to unite with, and to harmonise with sphere in its revolutions, I behold souls refuse to serve their fellow souls, and shrink from each other, languishing away in solitude and loneliness.

Oh, Master! wherefore should not all souls mutually enlighten each other, aid each other, unite with each other?

The words of complaint have risen to my lips, and it may be that I myself, in my own bounded sphere, it may be that I have opposed obstacles to this harmony.

It may be that I have never diffused exteriorly that light Thou hast implanted within me; it may be that I have never diffused it over others, as the sun reflects his luminous rays over the mountains' sides.

It may be that I have denied myself to many and many an intelligence that claimed my support.

It may be that I have never sought to emerge from my solitude, so as to unite with one of those in that union which acquires strength each succeeding day, which men and the things of time cannot destroy, that union whose invisible bond eternity itself shall tend to develop and fortify.

O Thou, whom I name my Master, do Thou say to my soul how she may cast her light over other spirits, how she may aid them, how she may unite with them.

O, teach her the secret of this harmony, the necessary prelude to one still grander, which I shall find one day in a new earth and in new heavens.

Before the hour of transformation, I aspire to come forth from my solitude, I desire to live; but, in order to live, I must love, for he who loves not abides in death.

To enlighten souls, to aid them, to unite with them—it is to love them in Thee—it is to love Thee Thyself.

Oh, Master! do Thou bestow on me the science of love.

The Master.—My son, I have listened to thy plaint, I have heard thy prayer; behold Me.

Thou art sad, and thy sadness shall endure so long as this earth will not have been purified by fire.

The spheres enlighten each other, and they unite and produce that harmony which ravishes thee, because they obey *Him who Is*.

Constrained to submit, not one amongst them revolts or utters a discordant sound.

But, so is it not with this people of souls that moves around thee, for those souls are free.

They are free, and, accordingly as they employ their liberty, the harmony subsists, or else disappears.

They are free to love, or not to love, the principle of all love.

But there is a chastisement which reaches them when they turn aside from this principle; and this chastisement is that of dispersion.

Truly, truly, do I say unto thee, souls do not enlighten each other mutually, forasmuch as they seek not the true light.

They combine not, they aid not each other, because they remove from the infinite love.

Wouldst thou establish harmony amongst these souls; do thou commence by establishing it betwixt thyself and Me.

The work of uniting souls to God, and of uniting them amongst themselves, is one which demands light and force from on high.

Now, I tell thee, he who abides not in union with Me through love, abides in darkness and in weakness.

I am the true light which enlightens all men, coming into the world; and it is for this that My Father made Me known from the beginning—that

My light might be diffused over all who would believe in Me.

I am the Word, that Word by which all things were made; and for this My Father revealed My force and My power from the commencement, that salvation might be given to all who would hope in Me.

And, therefore, do not thou undertake that task which demands light and force from on high, till thy heart shall have ascended towards Him who bestows that light and that force.

My son, give Me thy heart, and I shall render it strong.

As the tree that the husbandman would transplant, which bears no fruit before its roots have been hidden in the bosom of the earth, so thy heart cannot possess true love, before it has established on Me its everlasting resting place.

The branch must needs rest attached to its stem, that so it may not wither away, and the members of the body—that they may retain their principle of movement and force—may not be severed from their centre of life.

And thy heart, is it not like to the branch of the tree, to the members of the body?

Therefore, before all other things, do thou seek to know Me; for, I repeat it—he who knows Me, gives himself to Me, and, in so doing, he receives the true force in the only true love.

The Disciple.—Oh, Master! I desire that this heart should be Thine; do Thou aid me, do Thou grant that I may know Thee.

The Master.—Thou hast said it; in order to love, thou must know: listen, and I shall speak to thee of Myself.

I am the perfect image of My Father, the figure of His substance, and the splendour of *His glory*.

I am the Word, the eternal Word of the Father, the virtue and the wisdom of the Godhead, the first-born before all creatures.

I said, and all was done; I commanded, and all was executed.

I am He of whom it was said: Thou art My Son, sit Thou at My right hand; in My bosom Thou wast begotten before the day star.

My Father and I are one, and therefore am I the strong God, the splendour of the Eternal Light, the Father of the world to come, the Prince of Peace.

In Me are hidden all treasures of wisdom and of knowledge, because I am the only Son of God and the heir of all things.

And, therefore, has My Father given Me a name above all other names; that at this name every knee may bend, in heaven, and on earth, and in hell, and that every tongue may confess that I am truly in the glory of God My Father.

I walk on the clouds of heaven, and I come to commune with the ancient of days, and I receive power, and honour, and empire.

All nations, all tribes, and all tongues serve Me, and My power is an eternal power which may not be wrested from Me, and My kingdom shall never be destroyed.

The beauty of all things spiritual and corporeal in the universe has issued from My hands, and I am beauty in its essence—beauty unchangeable.

In Me are combined all degrees of loveliness that thine eye may behold distributed amongst creatures, and these attributes in Me surpass in nobleness all that is to be found in the most perfect of creatures.

I am the final end, the model of all things beautiful in creation, and all these things I call to Myself in order to perfect them, in reflecting on them the rays of My beauty.

I am the flower issuing from the root of Jesse, on which the Spirit has reposed, and all the plenitude of the Divinity dwells corporeally within Me: for it is written that My Father has not dealt out to Me the riches of the Spirit in weight and in measure, but—beyond all measure.

Glory and beauty are in My presence, sanctity and magnificence are within My sanctuary.

I am the loveliest amongst the children of men, and grace is diffused over My lips.

I have clothed Myself with splendour as with a garment, and I have done all things in perfection.

My word is living and efficacious; it is more penetrating than is a two-edged sword, it pierces into the most hidden folds of the mind and of the soul, it discovers all the thoughts and the movements of the heart.

All My words are as precious perfumes, and My tongue is full of suavity and delight, and torrents of sweetness flow from My lips.

O My son! let this first insight I have given thee into Myself not fall upon thy heart as upon an ungrateful soil.

There is, in the sun, in the moon, in the stars, in the diamonds and in the precious gems, a beauty which ravishes thee.

There dwells within inanimate bodies, within the plants and the trees, within the roses and the lilies, a beauty still lovelier, that wraps thy spirit in contemplation.

And, canst thou not love the Son of Man, before whom these beauties are as though they were not?

There is, in the animals that people the earth, in the birds of the air, and in the fishes of the deep, a beauty still greater, and in presence of which thine heart seems still more widely to dilate.

Thou lovest the loveliness of bodies united to immortal spirits, and thou dost love with a love of predilection the supernatural beauty of pure souls.

And He who is perfect in all manner of beauty, because He is the splendour of the Father, Him canst thou not admire?

O My son! listen on to Me.

I it was who loved thee first. Where wast thou when I laid the foundations of the world?

And where when casting forth My line I fixed its utmost bounds?

Thou wast not, and behold, already I loved thee.

Where wast thou when the stars of the morning praised Me in concert, and where when I set barriers to the deep sea to keep her in bond, when she would fain overflow in coming forth from My hands as from the bosom of her mother?

When I veiled her with a cloud as with a garment, and when I covered her over with obscurity, as one wraps the babe in swathing bands?

Where wast thou when I imprisoned her within the bounds I had marked out to her, and when I said unto her: "Thus far thou shalt come and no further; here thou shalt break the pride of thy billows?"

Thou wast not, and already I loved thee. And now, hast thou not seen My love display itself abroad, as do the blossoms unfolded by the beams of the early sun?

Hast thou not heard My word call thee forth from nothing, to crown thee with glory and honour, and place thee above the works of My hands?

I have formed thy body out of the slime of the earth; I have propped thy flesh with bones, and these I have, as it were, broken at regular distances.

They have each their special joints, whereby they are encased within each other, and I have bound them together by nerves and sinews.

Thy flesh I have covered with skin soft and tender; I have made it compact and smooth, that thy face may not seem as it were bloody.

I have created innumerable conduits that carry the blood to the extremities of thy body, and from these to the centre; so as that the blood, as it were, waters the body, as the rains moisten the earth.

Thy arms I have endowed with force, and thy hands with suppleness, and I have encased thy head in strong and hard bones.

I have bored thy skull in exact proportions, and I have distributed the nerves destined to the sensations produced within its various conduits.

Thy neck I have rendered more flexible than the reed, and firmer than the oak, so that it may incline on all sides, and straighten, as though formed of one only bone.

I have combined the chief sensations on thy face in an admirable order, and I have embellished it by the freshness of thy lips and the movements of thy mouth.

I have kindled within thine eyes a celestial flame, and I have covered them with lids, that so they may open and close.

I have pictured within them the earth and the sea, and the stars that roll in the immensity of space.

Is it not I who have diffused over thy face the breath of life: and that breath—have I not drawn it from Myself?

Have I not bestowed on thee sentiment and life, and with these intelligence and liberty?

Whence proceeds this spiritual, this invisible being, which, working incessantly within thee, embraces all creation in an instant's space, and mounts to the very heavens? Whence comes it? Answer Me.

The throbbings of thine existence, are they not the vibration of My life; and thy soul, is she not a word issuing from My lips?

I have rendered her mistress of her actions, so as that no creature can coerce her will.

I have impressed her with My image, in a manner more perfect than the hand of the moulder stamps on the bronze the resemblance of a man.

I have gifted her with the faculty of knowledge, that so she may elevate herself into the regions of truth, as the eagle soars on high by the force of his wings.

I have endowed her with love, that as knowing the truth she may love it, and that loving it she may find that joy that endures for eternity.

Whence comes it that this spiritual substance should be in intimate union with the earthly slime, out of which I formed thee by the labour of My hands?

Whence arises this? Answer Me.

Is it that this corporeal matter has been enabled to form a pact with the immaterial spirit? And the spirit, if as having made this pact with matter, wherefore can she not recall it to memory?

Is it not that I have united these two extremes in such a way, as that the spirit cannot will and the members not move to obey, or that the members cannot move without the spirit, at the same moment conceiving some thought of activity, of happiness, or of sadness?

My son, listen to Me:

I have bestowed on thee My gifts, and thou hast not given Me thine heart; and behold how, to aid thee in thy course, I assumed thy flesh and abode amongst men.

Possessing the form and the nature of God, I thought it not robbery to be equal to God; nevertheless, I annihilated Myself in assuming the form and the nature of the servant.

I rendered Myself like unto man; and I was by My outward semblance deemed as man, so as to prove to thee the extent of My love.

Thy spirit, subjected to the dominion of the senses, can alone conceive that which is material and sensible; and behold why I would not rest within the bosom of the Father, invisible to thy nature.

I have knocked at the door of thine heart, and I have broken that obstacle that impeded its love, in rendering Myself visible to thine eyes, and accessible to thy senses.

I would bow Myself down to thy nature, all carnal as it is, in opening thy heart to the salutary love of My humanity, that I might elevate it afterwards to a more spiritual love, to that of My divinity.

And behold how mountains have been levelled in My presence, and how the hardest of rocks have been riven.

I have seen them melt before My eyes as wax

in the furnace; the most rebellious of souls have been moulded to love, and they have rushed after the odour of My perfumes.

I am the Lamb that cancels the sins of the world, and in seeing, in touching Me, hast thou not seen, hast thou not touched the Man of Sorrows?

From the sole of My foot to the crown of My head, is there one spot which has not been torn?

Am I not He whose voice gives utterance to this lamentation, to this complaint: Oh, all ye who pass the way, behold Me, and judge if there be a sorrow equal to My sorrow?

The pains which I endured for thee and for thy brethren, do they not surpass all those which man can suffer, as the high mountains overtop the humble hills?

And these pangs, have they not penetrated all the members, all the senses of My body, and into My soul and her every power?

And thus it is I have compared them to a baptism and to a chalice—to a baptism of blood, to a chalice of bitterness.

You men may say to the worm and to corruption: You are my brother and my sister; and the Son of Man, may He not say to poverty and to misery: You are My Mother and My sister?

I passed amidst men doing good, and in return they heaped Me with injuries.

Some amongst them said of Me: that man is a blasphemer and a leader of sedition.

And others said: that man is a lover of good cheer, and is possessed by an evil spirit.

And others again said: that man is ignorant, He is an impostor and a madman.

All the senses, all the members of My body, were they not immersed in a baptism of sorrow?

The sneers of My enemies and the tears of My friends wearied Mine eyes; and calumnies and blasphemies drenched Mine ears.

My thirst was consuming beyond all measure; and yet that thirst was unallayed.

My head, crowned with a crown of thorns, became like to a fountain of blood; My cheeks were bruised with buffets, and My body laid open by the violence of blows was, as it were, only one vast wound.

Suffering penetrated My soul and all her faculties.

In beholding the iniquities of all men, was she not more harassed than a vessel assailed by the tempest, and abandoned in a night of storm to the fury of the billows?

All prevarications were laid on My head, and My repentance was immense and immeasurable.

Was I not afflicted for each and every man— for each and every sin?

And that affliction which arose from the entrails of My goodness and My mercy, was it not infinite?

And did I not sever that bond which united My soul to My body; did I not break it asunder by the effusion of My blood?

Thou wast not redeemed with gold or with silver, or with any other vile or perishable matter, but with the blood of the new covenant, which was shed for the remission of sins.

Behold and judge how much I loved thee by My sufferings; behold and judge how much I loved thee by My death.

Raise thine eyes to the heights of the heavens, plunge them into the depths of the abysses; search, and tell Me if there be within thee, around thee, a love equal to this My love.

II.

The Master.—My son, thou hast asked of Me that thou mightest know Me, and, behold, I have revealed Myself to thee; and now, having once hearkened to My voice, do not harden thy heart.

I have bound thee with the bonds of love, and I say unto thee, do thou not rend these bonds asunder.

It is written: If thy enemy be hungry, give him to eat; if he be thirsty, give him to drink; and in so doing thou wilt heap burning coals upon his head, and his frozen heart will be set on fire.

And have I not given thee to eat when thou wast hungry; have I not give thee to drink in thy thirst?

Are not My favours as a great heap of burning coals rising above thine head?

I created thee first by My word, and I created thee a second time in completing the work of thy redemption by the effusion of My blood.

And have I not opened thy heart to My love by My favours?

The most ferocious of beasts are tamed by benefits, the lion recognizes the hand that feeds him, and canst thou not thank the hand that serves thee?

The dog accompanies his master wheresoever he goes; he searches for him with perseverance, and defends him with courage: and why? because his master gives him each day his morsel of bread and his portion of water.

And thou, wouldst thou not walk in the footprints of Him who nourishes thy soul with a celestial manna, and who assuages thy thirst with that water which springs up to eternal life?

Thou lovest him who comes to visit thee in those hours when thou dost groan under the weight of some affliction; thou dost welcome his words, and when he takes his departure, thine eyes follow him afar, and thy soul is moved in recollecting all he has done for thee.

And wherefore wouldst thou not love Me equally, and even still more? Am I not He who said: Come to Me all you who are afflicted and heavily laden, and I shall refresh you.

Oh, My son! thou art he to whom I cry, thou art he to whom My words are addressed. I love all men who love Me, and he who is diligent in seeking Me shall find Me.

I manifest Myself readily to those who seek Me, I anticipate the wishes of those who desire Me, and I am the first to come and meet them.

He who rises in the morning to meet Me, will find Me without difficulty; for I shall sit at his door to await him.

The Disciple.—Oh, Master! my eyes have not seen Thee, neither have my ears heard Thee, how then shall I love Thee?

For, man, is he not carnal? And his senses must be struck so as to awaken his heart. Joy and sorrow, hatred and love, pass into his soul by the contact of external things. And am I not man?

If I beheld Thy divine face, I could not resist that vision, for I should contemplate the virtue of the Godhead, and the all-pure effusion of His brightness.

Did I but hear the sounds of Thy voice, I should retain that breath of life Thou hast given me, so as not to lose a single note of its divine harmony, and my soul, captivated by its charms, should thenceforth be susceptible alone of heavenly emotions.

O, Master! do Thou dispel those shadows that withhold the throbbings of my heart from seeking the true way; and then shall I prefer Thee to the dominions, to the thrones of monarchs.

I shall contemn all riches, and shall esteem them as dross. The most precious and the most sparkling of gems will seem to me as without price, the purest of gold and of silver tried in the furnace, shall be for me but as the lightest of sand.

Then shall I love Thee above beauty and health, then shall I choose Thee for my light; because Thou art that sole light that is never extinguished.

The Master.—My son, it is written, that one day thou shalt behold Me face to face, and that for the present hour thou canst see Me but through a cloud and in creatures, as though it were in a mirror.

Hope not, therefore, that I shall dispel all those shadows which seem to arrest the transports of thy heart.

Even as My invisible perfections, My eternal power, and My divinity, have become visible since the creation of the world, by the knowledge imparted through creatures, so even canst thou attain to My love, through means of created things.

When thou dost contemplate the beauty of the sun, of the moon, of the stars which I have suspended in the heavenly arch, that beauty does it produce within thee nought else save a feeling of sterile admiration?

When thine eyes rest on the earth where thou dwellest, on the trees of her forests, on her mountains, on the most hidden flower of her valleys, dost thou not feel a something move within the depths of thy soul?

When thou beholdest beauty in the face of a mortal creature, does not a sentiment of love awake within thy breast?

Now, I say unto thee in truth, in loving all these visible things, thou commencest to love the invisible presence of Him who created them.

Even as in each plant that grows out of this earth there reside germs invisible to thine eyes, and which the sun will hereafter bring into life, even so there dwells in the love that thou feelest for the beauty of visible things the germ of another love that the sun of My grace can render fertile within thee.

Wherefore, then, art thou sad? If I have gifted thy heart with the sentiment that inspires it with the love of the beautiful, shall I not perfect this My work?

I have disposed all creatures as do the children of men those steps that mount to the summit of the edifices which their hands erect, and I have done so that thou mayest ascend to Me through these same creatures.

I abide in the depths of each of My works, that I may give them life, and beauty, and force, and if thou seekest Me in My works, wilt thou not find Me?

I dwell in the colours that enchant thy sight, in the harmonious sounds that greet thine ear, and in the perfumes that delight thy senses.

External objects would possess no power over thee, and would produce neither joy or sorrow within thy soul, did I not endow them with that power.

Learn, then, to see My strength and My infinite power in the might and in the power of creatures, and in their beauty to contemplate My sovereign loveliness.

My son, he who seeks Me in the depths of the heavens and in the entrails of the earth, will find Me, but he who seeks Me within himself will perceive Me still more easily.

I am nigh to thee, and so nigh that I hear the most insensible murmur of thy lips; for it is in Me that thou art, it is in Me that thou livest.

I dwell in thee more perfectly than in other creatures; for I am within thee as in My image, and My temple wherein I would be loved and known.

My divine essence pervades thy whole body, and thy whole soul; it fills thee entirely; and in it My Father contemplates Himself, and in this contemplation He reproduces Me incessantly.

I am in thee as the sole principle of thy whole being, of thy whole knowledge, of all the power, of all the goodness thou mayest be endowed with.

Incline thine ear, and thou shalt hear Me, for that word that knocks at thy heart, to draw it towards the Sovereign Good, that word that knocks without ever tiring, is My word.

My voice sustains within thee the hope of a futurity of light and of joys ineffable, and it acts in contradiction with the vanity and the affliction of things present, which produce within thy soul nought save ineffectual suffering.

I speak, in order to check within thy heart the onset of evil passions, and to control it in presence of all transient and present happiness.

I speak, in order to excite within it salutary remorse; as the wind stirs up the waters of the sea, and swells them into mountains on its surface.

I speak, in order to detach thee from present advantages, lest thy soul should abandon herself to them with dangerous ardour, and suffer herself to be dried up, as a drop of water in the dust of the highways.

I speak all these various words, and thou dost hearken to them, because I am within the depths of thy soul, as in a germ that I would fain unfold to My image.

And now, if I be in each creature and in the depths of thy being, if thy spirit may touch Me within thee and around thee, wherefore shouldst thou say once more: O Master! how should I love Thee?

What matters it, even shouldst thou not see Me with thy corporeal eyes: thou dost love that spiritual essence which thou stylest thy soul, and yet, have thy corporeal eyes been enabled to distinguish it? Answer Me.

And this spirit of thine abides solely within thee; and am I not within thee, around thee, and within the centre of all creatures which exist apart from thy members and thy senses?

Rejoice, then, for I have placed Myself in the midst of thine heart—at the door of thy heart, so as that thou canst neither shut thyself up within thyself, or come forth from thyself without touching My divine essence, or treading on it on thy passage.

Rejoice thou, for, without having solicited Me, yea, even before thou couldst have asked Me, I disposed all things so as to render Myself accessible to thy love.

The Disciple.—O Master, I know that Thou art around me, and within me, that in Thee I live, in Thee I move, and in Thee I am; wherefore, then, does not my heart bound from its centre into Thee?

Wherefore does it give itself to things created and imperfect, and not to that which is uncreated and perfect? O Master! is there not herein some profound mystery?

The Master.—Truly, thou hast said it, for therein lies a great mystery; but be thou consoled, for thou shalt know whence this proceeds, and what power I have given thee over it.

My son, listen to Me! this mystery is thy own work, it proceeds from thee, as the child proceeds from the father, as the tree proceeds from the germ hidden in the bosom of the earth.

Thy soul will not fly towards Me, because she will not abandon self.

Self-love consumes—absorbs her; now, I tell thee, this evil divides her force, engenders her decomposition, and is the cause why she descends to nothingness.

And that soul that loses her force, and becomes decomposed in her substance—that soul, can she love?

Could the eagle, whose audacious flight thou admirest, could he launch into the air and hide himself in the clouds, were he to lose those plumes that give vigour to his wings?

There lurks within the depths of thy heart a secret love of self, and this it is which separates thee from Me, and arrests thy career, as the avalanche, falling from the mountain's side on the highway, arrests the course of the traveller, and severs him from that spot where he longed to take his repose.

Thyself thou dost prefer to order, to justice, to virtue, to thy fellow-men, to their happiness, to their welfare; and in this thy preference, dost thou not interpose an obstacle betwixt thyself and Me?

In the madness of thy love, dost thou not even go so far as to prefer thyself—in the enjoyment, which for thee can endure but an instant—to the joy that knows no end?

Thou seest that both suffering and remorse must result from that present joy which thou embracest with avidity; and that suffering, that remorse, do not restrain thee.

Descend into thine heart, and thou wilt find that frightful egotism that parches it up, revealing itself by its effects in thy spirit and in thy senses.

Thou art but a member of that great body of thinking beings which I created; and yet thou dost say: I would render myself both centre and body.

As thine eye, in contemplating objects material and visible, brings them within its focus, so as that they increase or disappear as they approach or recede from thee, even so, that which regards moral order and truth, appears to thy spirit as do visible objects to the eyes of thy body.

Then it is that pride declares itself, then it is that the egotism of the spirit unfolds itself, and that the thought of another does not seem to thee as luminous as thine own.

It is then thou dost live isolated, wrapped up in thine own intelligence, contemplating self alone, and as the sun, in rising above the horizon, interposes a dense veil betwixt thine eyes and the stars suspended in the firmament, even so does thy proper light efface and annihilate in thy regard all the lights of other men.

And that egotism of the spirit, that ill-governed love of thine own conceptions, how can it not but estrange thee from that common reason which I have diffused over the human race?

And if the wisdom of those who preceded thee, and whom thou dost style thy fathers, seems to thee but as vain, in the arrogance of thy spirit dost thou not wander still further from Me, who am the eternal reason and wisdom?

He who is held down by the weight of his body, and cannot climb the humble hill, can he reach the summit of the high mountain?

And My conceptions, and the doctrine of My words, are they not, in presence of human thoughts and of human doctrines, even as the high mountains compared to the humble hills?

If thou wilt not receive the light of thy brothers, how canst thou not but reject My light, which, emanating from on high, presents itself to thy spirit, charged with the deepest of mysteries?

In truth, I tell thee, the egotism of thine intelligence, in severing thee from the thoughts of other men, likewise severs thee from Me.

Borne away by a secret and ill-ordained love, thou renderest thyself not alone the centre and principle in regard to lights partial and bounded, but thou wouldst yet remain both centre and principle, regarding the Infinite Truth and the principle of light.

I am within thee and around thee; and yet thou art sad because thy soul cannot behold Me; but let thy sadness and thy complaints fall back on thyself:

Descend once more into thine own heart, and thou wilt find that frightful egotism which parches it up, revealing itself in its effects, not alone in thy spirit, but in thy very senses.

I have kindled within thee a fire—a fire that gives impulsion to thy will, that fertilizes thy blood, and that gives force to thy members.

And hast thou not before the time abused the

power of that fire, so that at present it consumes all, and scorches up thy existence in all its germs, in all its roots?

And when the time arrived, did not the egotism of thy senses repel the intermittence of that flame, in giving it a continuity and an intensity which destroyed the new forces arising within thee?

Thy soul must needs retain all her power, all her energy, with the purity of her affections, that she may unite with Me; and the egotism of the senses has banished from her all enthusiasm with all wisdom and love.

That fire, destined to produce holy emotions and sublime affections, that fire, turned aside from its proper destination, has consumed thee entirely in thy germ and in thy bloom.

It has diffused itself over thy heart as a flood of burning lava over a fertile field, and thy heart is now but as ashes.

Within thee is a void, and thou hast grown hard like the rock, and frozen like the wave that has shivered beneath the breath of the wintry wind.

Thy very senses, fatigued and exhausted by the fury of thy egotism, have become weakened, as those of him whose hair is whitened by time.

There is now within thee nought save death—death in thy spirit, death within thine own body, death everywhere.

And where now, where wilt thou take this flood of life which may bear thee on to Me, as the waves of the sea bear the ship to its harbour?

If matter has dried up the sources of purity, of pity, of charity, and of love, if matter itself has become annihilated beneath its own weight, how then shouldst thou not be in My presence as a being without life, and as one incapable of a thought, of an aspiration, of a movement?

Thy senses have in their fury drunk up the last drop of blood remaining in thy heart, so that thou canst no longer love any save those thine eyes behold or thine hands can touch.

How then canst thou rush with holy impulse towards Him who is invisible to corporeal eyes, and inaccessible to hands of clay?

A soul, in her strength, in her beauty, in her light, and in her love, cannot bound from her centre and unite with Me, if I do not descend to her by My grace.

And how can it be with a soul that has lost all energy, all beauty, all light, and all love?

And now, what may I effect with a ruin? for art thou not like to a great edifice whose wreck is alone visible?

Does the painter essay to trace lines on the tattered canvass, or can the artist awaken harmonious sounds on the riven chords of a lyre?

O, My son! re-establish order within thyself, recover back those gems which were once thy splendour, and which the egotism of the spirit and of the senses has strewn one after the other on the highway.

Cast forth that pride in which thou didst lie

buried as within a sepulchre, and so thou shalt regain thy first strength with thy first beauty.

Shake off the tyranny of thy senses, and so thou canst once more unfold in true love thy whole soul to My vivifying and living image.

Have confidence, for, behold, already have I pronounced over thee a word of resurrection.

III.

The Disciple.—O, Master! I have comprehended that I had wandered from the true love by the inordinate love of self.

I have conceived that my soul, abandoned to decomposition by the abuse of light, and by the egotism of the senses, had become incapable of receiving that grace which was destined to constitute the bond of her union with Thee.

And, comprehending this, I have seen why I had abandoned my heart to things created and imperfect, and I have discovered the source of that mystery whose depths overwhelmed my mind.

O, Master! Thou hast told me that I shall know that power which Thou hast given me over this mystery of iniquity, of which I am myself the first cause.

Do Thou console Thy servant, and, after having revealed to him the knowledge of evil, teach him to break that obstacle which severs him from Thee.

The Master.—My son, he who is desirous to see Me, and to give Me his heart, must first die; for it is written, that no one can live and see God.

And, behold! this is the word of resurrection which I have announced, which I have pronounced over thee.

Even as the grain of seed, which cannot unfold itself or produce a plant or a tree charged with flowers and fruits, if it do not first die in the earth, even so thou canst not form and develop within thy soul the true love, save by means of death.

Death means to say, sacrifice; and sacrifice is the act whereby man quits self and his actual state in order to ascend incessantly towards the Infinite.

To enter into the way of sacrifice, it is to retire from the exterior world, within one's self, and soar from thence to all that is most elevated; it is to submit the spirit to the Most High, and the flesh to the spirit, to quit the body, and to enter into self, so as to obey order.

No other passage is there from darkness to light, no other way from the impure to the pure.

My eternal wisdom is hidden from the eyes of those who distract themselves amidst the perishable objects that surround them; and, in order to unite the finite with the Infinite, the creature with the Creator, they must necessarily submit the one to the other.

These perishable objects, on which thou exhaustest thy soul, speak to thee of truth and of happiness; and wheresoever thou hearest their voice, it is My word that strikes upon thine ear.

But, whence is it that thou dost so ill comprehend their language? And, knowest thou not, that if they speak to thee of a flitting happiness, it is to kindle within thee a holy thirst of an eternal, of an infinite felicity?

These objects I have invested with charms, and with beauty, in order to lay within thine heart a foundation of love, and I have left in them defects, and I have set limits to their charms and to their beauty, so as to conduct thee, by means of these limits and these imperfections, to the Sovereign love.

Wherefore, then, wouldst thou impede the development of thy entire being, in refusing to listen to My word in that of these mortal creatures?

The Disciple.—O, Master! I have suffered myself to be taken in the snare, as the bird in the nets of the huntsman.

And how shall I abandon a limited satisfaction to seek for that which is infinite? And how shall I be enabled to die in giving Thee my present force, and my very self, that I may find Thee?

Is there within me, or near me, some force which can struggle against the egotism of this spirit and of this heart? If thus it be, do Thou show me this force.

The Master.—My son, there is within thee a Divine sense which combats thy egotism, inasmuch as this sense proceeds from Me; and I have given it thee, to the end that, as serving to sustain thy will, thou mayest consummate the holocaust, and ascend to the love of heavenly things.

Even as there exists a force which determines an irresistible attraction betwixt bodies, so is there likewise, in beings capable of love, a force that attracts them to the Sovereign Good.

That force which stirs within thee, in order to detach thee from all manner of anguish and of torture, from all deception and vanity, that force is My voice; it is in Me thou art, it is in Me thou livest.

And that sanctuary wherein I speak, and wherein mortal man may not enter, that sanctuary is conscience.

Conscience is the place of refuge wherein I am found, forasmuch as I am in the midst of the soul, and My throne is in the conscience of the good.

Even as thy spirit cannot pass from the view of things finite to that of the infinite, without having the implicit perception of the latter, so in like manner thy will has need of the implicit love of the Almighty, in order to pass from love finite to the love of Me.

And now, do thou rejoice, for I have given to thy will that which it needed, even as I have given sustenance to all beings endowed with movement and life.

Rejoice, for sustained by Me thou canst rend asunder those bonds which retain thy soul captive to egotism; thou canst renounce all things perishable; and thou canst renounce thyself that thou mayest find Me.

Knowest thou not that thy soul bears within herself the truth, and that it suffices for her to unfold her fibres, to open her bosom, and to develop her force that she may comprehend Me?

Knowest thou not that in thy soul there is a point which is the centre and the summit of her rays, and that in this centre she imperceptibly finds herself united to Me by a profound and mysterious contact?

Truly, truly, do I say unto thee, the chief means whereby thou mayest consummate the holocaust which I demand of thee, this means is within thee, forasmuch as conscience is given thee.

O, My son, let conscience be thy altar.

The Disciple.—O, Master! I have comprehended that I should penetrate into myself so as to find that victim which might glorify Thee.

I have understood that I should die to myself; I have understood that the divine sense Thou hast placed within my soul, was given me so as to consummate the sacrifice.

And, behold! I tremble before the holocaust, for I said: shall not the sacrifice of the will be its utter annihilation? shall not that sacrifice be its enslavement?

O, Master! in order to attain this Thy love, is there need of the annihilation of my soul, and not of her expansion? is there need of servitude, and not of liberty?

The Master.—My son, disquiet not thyself; I have spoken to thee of holocaust and of death, but not of annihilation and of slavery.

To sacrifice thy will means not to annihilate it, but to disengage it from those bonds which impede its ardour; it is not to plunge it into slavery, but to render it free.

He who truly loves Me concentrates all the energies of his soul, of which he dissipates not a single particle, and his love augments incessantly.

Now, I tell thee, whosoever will not consummate the holocaust which I demand, will not concentrate, but he will divide the energies of his soul, and thus dividing them, he will fetter and not expand himself.

Even as the stars, and the sun, and the earth, and the trees, and the plants, and all the works of My hands, are but finite creatures, even so thy soul, thy mind, and thy heart, and all that is spiritual within thee, are likewise finite.

Behold how thy will is finite; at times it desires with energy, but, so soon as an obstacle is interposed, does it not grow discouraged?

It has commenced by desiring with ardour; yet, a little while, and behold it wills less strongly, and the hour comes when, vanquished by its own weakness, it wills no longer.

· And when an obstacle presents itself, dost thou not feel that it is arrested by the very goal it has just attained, by that advantage which it sought after, as is a courier by the barrier he cannot surmount?

It pursues a present joy, but does this, when attained, prove an aid in advancing it in its onward, in its upward career? Do thou beware of believing this. It is nothing more than a barrier it has placed in its path.

Thy will, bound up within itself, is by far more finite than those natural objects which thine eyes can contemplate, and which thine hands can touch.

Behold the stars, and the earth, and the mountains, and the plants, and the water, and the fire; all these objects, in their grandeur and in their lustre, are finite, yet they have their plenitude.

And that will of thine, does it equal these in permanence and in unity? And does it possess itself completely in radiating like them on all sides, and at all times?

In its action, dost thou not see it attach itself to one sole point, unmindful of all others, and become exclusive whilst proceeding onwards in its single course?

Thy will is finite in light and in force, it is broken and captive; wherefore, then, fearest thou to sacrifice it?

Wouldst thou not annihilate it, didst thou leave it in its actual state? Forasmuch as, falling back on things finite and on itself, should it not oppose an obstacle to its own dilatation?

Wherefore dreadest thou the sacrifice? To sacrifice thy will, is it not to retrench those desires, evil and useless and vain, which entangle thee within their folds, as the reptile coils around some body, that he may deposit within it his venom?

Did not the wise man utter this prayer: O Lord, my God, Father of my life, remove from me all desire?

In retrenching all vain and unavailing desires, dost thou not remove from thy heart those troubles and disquietudes that come to afflict it, and dost thou not fill thy soul with a holy peace?

Desires are fertile in suffering, and the more they multiply within the heart of man, the more they augment its tribulations.

As, in order to extinguish a fire, one removes the wood and all other combustible materials of which it is composed, so, in like manner, one cannot extinguish that consuming fire which saddens the soul, and plunges her into bitterness, save in subduing the desires of the will.

To hope with ardour for that which perishes, it is to render oneself the slave of hope; to dread beyond measure that which, as being terrestrial, can only afflict the body, is another slavery.

He who hopes—does he possess himself? He who fears, is he himself? or does his heart not drag a chain which binds it captive?

Wherefore dost thou dread the sacrifice? To sacrifice thy will, is it not to rend asunder that bond which binds thee to mortal creatures, that thou mayest undertake all things with a spirit free and disengaged?

When thou givest thy heart, does it not cease to belong to thee; and if thou art no longer its master, how mayest thou constrain it to obey better inspirations?

The inordinate love of the most insignificant of creatures checks the career of the heart, as the cable arrests the course of the ship; it becomes like to a thick wall, which, receiving the sun's rays, will not permit them to pass through.

And these same creatures, what can they effect for thy happiness? what recompense dost thou await in return for that love thou dost bestow on them?

Can all the advantages they possess, can they fill the hand of the smallest child?

Knowest thou not that it is written: The slaves of this world, devoid of judgment and of sense, have passed the night of this life as in a sleep.

Nought remains to them of all that which they had seen in their dream, because I have annihilated the pomp of their imagined grandeur.

All has vanished away from before them as a flitting dream, all has disappeared as a vision of the night.

All those goods conferred by creatures are like to a shadow, and they who possess them say within themselves at the hour of their awakening: What have availed unto us honours, and pride, and abundance, and riches? All has glided away as a vapour.

Truly, truly do I say unto thee, that man passes his life in the midst of images and of shadows, and he who believes himself rich grasps but the semblance of true riches, and he who enjoys glory possesses but its image.

Learn, then, that there are two worlds, the one wherein dwell truth and things in their proper nature, and the other wherein all things exist but as in symbol.

What value can those goods possess which thou seekest, and with which thou art captivated? Knowest thou not that thy celestial Father distributes them to those who rejoice in iniquity, and to the most perverse of men?

And now, does a king hold in high estimation those things he gives to his enemies? Did he value them highly, would he not deny them to those?

The joy thou dost demand of these perishable goods oftentimes sickens thy heart, and will never content it; for, it is written, that the covetous will never possess riches sufficient to render them satisfied.

And, if thus it be with the riches of the avaricious, so is it likewise with all those other goods, for the heart of him who seeks them.

Whosoever drinks of this water shall be again thirsty, for it is not within its power to refresh the ardour of the soul, which can find no repose save in the Infinite.

Did not Solomon, in his glory, experience in all those goods he had received trouble and affliction of spirit; and in the sorrow of his heart, did he not exclaim : Vanity of vanities, and all the things of this earth are but vanity?

Can all those advantages which creatures bestow render thee worthy; and if it be not so, are they not ills rather than advantages?

Where is the rich man who does not place his confidence in his treasures? where is he? that we may extol him.

He who has elevated himself above his brothers, and whose arm has become powerful, takes complacency in his grandeur, and despises the little and the weak; forasmuch as he says within his heart: "I am not as other men."

He who lives in delight, and whose senses are ever covetous of new satisfactions, grows hard-hearted and pitiless; he witnesses the misery, the affliction of his brother, and he seeks not to succour it; for he has said within his heart: "Let us shun the house of mourning: better is it to enter the abode of festivity."

As the most robust health can scarcely withstand the violence of poison, even so the most vigorous soul resists with difficulty the ordeal of those temptations proceeding from the evils which flesh and blood style real advantages.

If thou canst not as yet so estimate them, open thine eyes to the light, and behold at least how rapidly they glide away.

They escape from thy grasp at each hour of the day; thou seizest on them anew, and they escape once more, and scarcely is it given thee to possess them one instant without disquietude and dread.

And even shouldst thou enjoy them in their plenitude during thy whole life, would they not still pass away with rapidity?

Thy life is a vapour, which, rising from the earth, appears for a short space, quickly to disappear; it is but as a light wind that passes away.

And, if thus it be with thine existence, how can it be otherwise with all those goods which seduce thy will and hold it captive?

Knowest thou not, that since man has been on this earth, it has been at all times true that adulation, glory, the satisfactions and the pleasures of sinners and of worldlings, have been but as things that flit away? Their grandeur has been but as a point, and their duration but for an instant.

Wherefore shouldst thou dread sacrifice? To sacrifice thy will, it is to unite it to Mine; to will as I will; it is to will with Me, to will in Me.

And thus to unite it, is it not to glorify it? is it not to develop it in light and in force?

My will is infinite in light, for My eyes are more luminous than the sun.

I know Myself thoroughly, because I am ever present to Myself, and nothing can hinder Me from comprehending Myself.

I know all My creatures with this same plenitude, for I am their Creator, and I might not create them without knowing them.

I know their essence and their relations with other creatures, because it is My will that has allotted to all beings their several states; it is My will which has fixed their destination, their co-ordination with respect to each other, in assigning to each of them the place which it holds.

My will is infinite in light, for it is written of Me: "That I am the God of all science, and that I discover the traces of that which was most hidden."

And do I not call those beings that do not exist, even as I do those which are already?

My knowledge extends over all possible things, for they are alone possible in virtue of that power I possess to create them, and without knowing them I may not create them.

My knowledge extends over all things past, for they have had existence but through My will; but it likewise extends over things present, for these latter exist but through that same will.

I know all future events that will necessarily occur, because all passes, relatively to Me, in the space of a single indivisible instant; and I see in the future those very things that depend on thy free will.

I sound thine heart, and I read in thy soul the most secret thoughts that move her, because for Me there are no secret thoughts, and nothing is hidden from My perception.

I behold all the ways of men, I pierce the depth of the abysses, I penetrate into the most hidden places.

Wherefore shouldst thou dread to unite thy will to Mine? My will is infinite in light, and is it not equally infinite in force?

I will, and the pure spirits issue out of nothing, to adore and to serve Me; I will, and the spiritual essence combines with the material substance; I will, and the corporeal substance rests alone as a man devoid of movement and intelligence.

The boundless force of My will shines forth in each of My works, for they subsist and endure throughout all ages, and they obey all My commands.

I have darted My kindling glance into the firmament, and it is I who enlighten the world from the heights of the heavens.

The stars follow the course I have assigned to them, they hold themselves ready to obey My behest, and they are indefatigable in their watchings.

I open My treasures, and I launch the lightnings for the execution of My judgments.

Like unto a flock of birds, the vapours fly at My command; I condense the clouds, and from them I send down the hail like stones.

By one glance of Mine eye I make the mountains quake; and by one act of My will I raise the wind of the south.

I strike the earth by the din of My thunder, and by the tempest of the north wind, and by the fury of the whirlwinds.

I spread abroad the snow, as though a multitude of birds that alight on the plain, or a cloud of locusts that descends upon the earth.

When I bid the cold north wind to blow, the water freezes, as it were, into crystal, and the ice covers all the mass of waters as with a coat of mail.

I will the bread to come forth from the earth, and the wine that rejoices the heart of man; I water the trees of the plains, as well as the cedars of Lebanon, by the abundance of the rains.

Seek in the heavens, on the earth, in the regions below, one creature who can resist My will, and do thou lead him into My presence.

Search for that barrier which My will cannot surmount, for that obstacle it cannot resist, and do thou show Me that barrier, show Me that obstacle.

Why shouldst thou dread to unite thy will to Mine? Inasmuch as Mine is infinite in light and in force, is it not alike infinite in perseverance?

I exist necessarily, and he who is necessarily that which he is, cannot have discordant thoughts or a discordant will. Ever the same, I always will, I always effect the same things.

Thy will is finite in perseverance, because thy spirit discovers incessantly truths which were unknown to it, as well as new motives of action; but thus it is not with My will, because so it is not with My Spirit.

That which exists, exists because so I will; and that which I will, I will from all eternity. Do thou not admit the belief that those changes that occur in this visible universe, are the effects of different and successive acts of My will.

In eternity is there succession, and can it find place in the thoughts of Him who is eternal?

All those vicissitudes thou seest in the universe proceed from My continued and persistant will, which has ordained them all at the same time, and by one single decree.

One fixed cause, does it not oftentimes produce effects successive and varied? At the same moment, and by the same action, dost thou not see the sun enlighten one object and heat another; delight the eye that is healthy, and fatigue another which is unsound?

Now, I tell thee, thus is it with Me: I have assigned to all My creatures laws that cause them to execute all those revolutions through which they pass, but those laws proceed from a will persevering and immutable.

I am not as the children of men, who abandon one thought to fix on another, as one casts away a worn out garment to assume a fresh one.

I am ever the same, because incapable of change, or the shadow of a vicissitude.

Wherefore shouldst thou dread to unite thy will to Mine? My will, infinite in light, in force, and in perseverance, is it not likewise infinite in liberty?

I am independent of all creatures, and he who is independent can experience no manner of contrariety.

The beings I have drawn forth from nothing

have not forced Me to create them, for they did not as yet exist, and My own nature did not constrain Me to launch the worlds into the regions of space.

In all the works of My hands, dost thou not discern a counsel, a design, and seest thou not an end, and a means adapted to this end?

And, if thus it be, how shouldst thou not be necessitated to believe that it is a free will that has regulated this order?

He who acts from necessity, has he the power of determining himself, or can he propose to himself an end, and choose the means for its attainment?

Say not that I, as being immutable, My will, in virtue of this immutability, cannot be infinite in liberty, and desire this thing and that other.

Knowest thou not, that in that indivisible instant that composes an entire eternity, I freely will all that which exists; and that I cannot change, for this reason, that there are no other instants during which this change may be effected?

I have done that which I willed in heaven, on earth, on the deep, and in the very depths of the abysses, and in My eternity having freely ordained all beings and all events, I have made of My liberty all that use I would fain make.

Though My actual will may seem to thee a thing of necessity, yet it is not so in an absolute degree, inasmuch as it is the necessary consequence of My primary volition freely conceived.

I am infinite in My liberty, as I am in My

power, for it is written of Me: "That I have done all things according to the counsel of My will."

Wherefore wouldst thou still dread to unite thy will to Mine?

My will, infinite in light, in force, in perseverance, in liberty, is it not likewise infinite in all its greatness?

It radiates on all sides, it radiates unceasingly, it possesses itself entirely in its unity, and in its infinite plenitude, inasmuch as there can be neither time nor place in My regard.

I do not stand without the precincts of the world, neither am I confined within them; and when I act upon time, and the mutations of created things, I am not, as a necessary consequence, in any time whatsoever, or in any change of being.

I have gifted with succession the bounded existence of My creatures, and, nevertheless, at no given time have I been creating certain beings rather than others.

I am eternally creating that which is created this day, as I am eternally creating that which was created on the day when I fixed the sun and the stars in the heights of the heavens.

Consider all created things, and thou wilt see that the one is more ancient than the other, that this one is vaster than that other; but, for Me, I am immense in each of them, in the least as in the greatest.

I am higher than the heavens, deeper than hell,

longer than the earth, and broader than the ocean; and if it be thus, how may it be that My will is but a fraction of itself?

How may it be that it cannot diffuse its rays on all sides, that it should become exclusive in concentrating itself in one direction, that it should be productive on this point and sterile on that other?

Whither canst thou go that thou mayest not encounter it? Dost thou mount to the heavens, thou shalt find it. If thou descendest into the depths of the regions below, thou shalt still find it.

Man of little faith, wherefore dost thou fear? Is it then thy annihilation I desire, when I speak of holocaust? Is it, then, a servitude I impose in demanding the union of thy finite will with the will infinite?

The stalks of the vine bend earthwards, when finding no stay around them, but, so is it not when they may entwine themselves around the stem of the forest tree.

It is then they unfold themselves and grow vigorous, as the branches of the oak that is planted in a fertile ground.

And so is it with thy will. Alone and unsustained, it sinks beneath the weight of its own weakness, but, united to Mine, it becomes developed in force, in perseverance, in liberty, and in light.

Wouldst thou, then, advance forwards from light unto light? from slavery to independence, do thou consummate the sacrifice, and the sacrifice will bring with it a light, and an energy, and a wisdom ever increasing.

Then wilt thou listen to Me, then will the tumult of things created and imperfect have ceased to resound in thine ears.

It is then that, disengaged from the bonds that enchained thy will to things finite, thou shalt advance towards the Infinite with still greater rapidity than the great rivers rush towards the ocean.

Thou shalt then will with Me, and like Me, and thus willing, thy heart, expanded by the celestial aliment of obedience, shall enter into the joy of the true love.

IV.

The Disciple.—O, my Master! I return Thee thanks, forasmuch as Thou hast caused all fear to vanish from my heart.

To-day I begin to comprehend the sense of these words of Thine: "He who will not die to his own life cannot be My disciple."

I distinguish in this word a new birth for him who carries it into effect, and the consolation derived from this second birth.

I discern in this word the expansion of a will disengaged from all things finite, the transition from an existence bounded and sterile to another existence which is fertile and vast.

4

O, Master! Thou hast said to me, that to sacrifice my will was to unite it to Thine; and now, grant that my spirit may comprehend in what consists this union.

I have yearned to be enabled to say this word: It is no longer I who live, but it is Thou who livest in me. Do Thou hasten the accomplishment of my desires, for, behold, I have said: "Lord, what willest Thou of me?"

The Master.—If thou wilt unite thy will to Mine, then shalt thou complete this union; for My will is not hidden from thine eyes, as is the ineffable splendour of My divine essence.

I have manifested it to thee in My word, and My word is My law.

Now, I say unto thee: "Do thou fulfil My precepts, and so thou shalt find that union which thou seekest."

O, My son! behold how My commandments are the expression of My sovereign, of My infinite will, and these commandments, have I not sanctioned them by recompences and by chastisements?

I have promised to him who observes them a joy which will have no end. He shall see Me one day, not through symbols, or in mortal creatures, as it were in a mirror.

He shall contemplate Me such as I am, face to face: he shall know Me as I know him. It is in My light that he shall behold the light, and that light shall not be followed by night, nor obscured by the shadow of a cloud.

I shall be Myself his recompence, and he shall be satisfied to the fullest when he shall discover all My glory.

I shall dry up his tears, and I shall feast him from the abundance of My mansion, and I shall give him to drink of the torrent of My delights.

He shall see that which the eye of man cannot see; he shall hear that which the ear of man cannot hear, and his heart shall be filled with a joy which the heart of man has never felt.

And, now, if My commandments be the expression of My sovereign, of My infinite will, because I have promised to him who fulfils them that he shall enter into My joys, are they not still more the expression of My will, as having menaced with eternal chastisements him who despises them?

The wicked have said in the wanderings of their imagination: "The time of our life is short and tedious, and in the end of a man there is no remedy; and no man hath been known to have returned from hell.

"For we are born of nothing, and after this we shall be as if we had not been; for the breath in our nostrils is smoke, and speech a spark to move our hearts.

"Which, being put out, our body shall be ashes, and our spirit shall be poured abroad as soft air, and our life shall pass away as the trace of a cloud, and shall be dispersed in a mist which is driven away by the beams of the sun, and overpowered with the heat thereof."

They have said: "Our time is as the passing of a shadow, and there is no going back of our end; for it is fast sealed, and no man returneth.

"Come, therefore, and let us enjoy the good things that are present, and let us speedily use the creatures of our youth.

"Let us crown ourselves with roses before they are withered, let no meadow escape our riot."

They have said, moreover: "Let us oppress the poor just man, and not spare the widow, nor honour the ancient grey hairs of the aged.

"Let us, therefore, lie in wait for the just, because he is not for our turn, and he is contrary to our doings, and upbraideth us with transgressions of the laws, and divulgeth against us the sins of our way of life."

These things they have said. But I shall desperse their assembly as tow, and their end shall be to be consumed by fire.

And they shall fall after this without honour, and be a reproach among the dead for ever, for I shall burst them, puffed up and speechless, and shall shake them from the foundations, and they shall be utterly laid waste; they shall be in sorrow, and their memory shall perish.

They shall come with fear at the thought of their sins, and their iniquities shall stand against them to convict them.

And they shall be troubled with terrible fear. And My zeal will take armour, and I will arm the creature for the revenge of My enemies.

I will put on justice as a breast-plate, and will take true judgment instead of a helmet.

I will take equity for an invincible shield.

I will sharpen My severe wrath for a spear, and the whole world shall fight with Me against the unwise.

Then shafts of lightning shall go directly from the clouds; as from a bow well bent they shall be shot out, and shall fly to the mark.

O, My son! I have revealed to thee the recompences that attend the observance of My law, and the chastisement I reserve for those who despise it; and it is to this end, that thou mayest know where My will is to be found.

I have now fixed the wanderings of thy spirit; I have dispelled its disquietudes in displaying to thine eyes a marvellous light.

Do thou seek before all things to know My word, and when thou wilt have attained this knowledge, do thou retain it with fidelity.

My word is a lamp to thy feet, and a light to thy paths.

My precepts are the passage from the narrow and barren life to that life which is broad and fruitful, forasmuch as they shall constitute the bond of union between thy will and Mine.

Let thine eyes from the day-break turn to My law; for I have commanded thee to observe its testimonies as being essentially both justice and truth.

Hate all iniquity, and hold it in abhorrence, and praise Me seven times in the day for the judgments of My justice; for much peace have they who love My law.

Lean on My judgments, that thou mayest not wander in the wilderness, as a sheep that has gone astray; and rejoice in My commandments, as one who has found great and rich spoils.

My son, hear Me on. My will, signified to thee by My commandments, is likewise made known to thee by the joys and the sufferings that fill thine existence.

All that which happens in this world, with the exception of evil, is an effect of My will.

As I make My sun to rise in order to enlighten thee, as I make the earth produce those aliments that sustain thy body, as I contract thy members by cold and dilate them by genial heat, so likewise do I visit the sons of men with joy and with suffering.

The most insignificant as well as the greatest of events, are the perfect expression of My infinite will, for not a sparrow can fall to the earth independently of My will, and the very hairs of thy head are numbered.

And, now, I say unto thee in truth: it suffices not to accept joy, or to endure suffering, that thy will may be united to Mine.

Thou must needs receive the one and endure the other, in willing that which I will, and as I will it.

There are some, who, in accepting joy, will not that which I will, forasmuch as they receive it ill.

I bestow on them peace, with happiness in peace, and their hearts are unmoved by a sentiment of gratitude or love.

They accept joy as a something that is due to them, without disquieting themselves regarding the use to which they should convert it, and the profit which they should derive from it.

There are others, again, who, in accepting it, will it not as I will it, and those say within themselves: "Wherefore this joy? It is not that which I coveted; the joy which I sought not comes to me; and that which I sought after comes not."

And, further, they say within themselves: "Wherefore this incomplete joy? I coveted a complete satisfaction, and I received but a small portion; that felicity which falls to my lot is but a partial one."

O, My son! do thou not imitate those who hold this language in the depths of their hearts; for I tell thee, these, in receiving joy, unite not their will to Mine.

In thy happiness, seek not the happiness in itself, but that which I will in bestowing it on thee.

That which I will is the development of the true life within thee, and, therefore, do thou accept the present joy as the chief stay of that development.

Its mission, is it not to aid thee in ascending those heights where burns a light more brilliant, and where souls breathe an air more pure?

Say not thou: "Wherefore this joy? it is not that which I ambitioned." He who sounds the hearts and the loins, does He not know better than thou dost, the joy which is needful to thy heart, so as to advance it in the ways of wisdom?

And, moreover, say not: "Why this incomplete happiness?" Has the moment of perfect bliss arrived? This thou must merit, and it is for this reason that partial happiness is conceded to thee.

There are some who in enduring suffering do not will that which I will, for they ill sustain their tribulation.

I try them in order to humble them, and they, as not loving humiliation, listen but to the voice of the flesh that rebels against the trial.

And those say within themselves: "Our hands are not sullied, yet the Almighty chastises us as though we were men of iniquity.

"Perish the day of our birth, and let the moment of our creation be not counted amongst propitious moments.

"Let that day be changed into darkness, and let the Almighty from the heights of heaven regard it as though it had never been, let it cease to be enlightened by the sun's beams.

"Let a whirlwind of darkness envelop that night, let it not be reckoned henceforth amongst the days of the year, nor amongst the number of the months.

"Let the stars that should lighten it be obscured by its blackness; let it await the light, and let it not behold it; and let the dawn, when it glimmers, not arise upon it.

"Wherefore did we not die in our mother's entrails? Why did we not cease to live in issuing from them?

"Wherefore did they who received us at our birth, wherefore did they hold us upon their knees, and why did they nourish us with their milk?"

Thus they speak, and it is not that they may manifest the excess of their ills, but it is that they may satisfy an insensate rage; for they will not say within themselves: "We know, in truth, that man, if compared with God, shall not be justified."

They will not say within themselves: "Who are we, to presume to reply to Him? and who are we, to presume to address Him? Even were there within us some trace of justice, we should not reply, but we should conjure Him to pardon us."

They say not: "If we undertake to justify ourselves our own lips will condemn us; and if we desire to prove that we are innocent, He will convince us of sin."

Do thou beware of imitating those who hold not this language, for I say to thee in truth: those men in suffering do not unite their will to Mine.

He who so does, grows not angry, and sullies not his lips with cries of revolt, because he knows that I prepare hours of trial in My wisdom and in My love.

I have said: "Blessed are they who mourn, for they shall be comforted;" and I have said: "Blessed are they who suffer persecution for justice sake, for theirs is the kingdom of heaven;" and do thou rightly understand these words.

Have I not ordained each sadness and each sorrow with which I visit the children of men, to the end that they may contribute to My glory, and to their felicity?

I visit thee with the wind of tribulation, in order to enlighten thy soul regarding the evil which consumes it, in order to dissipate those external objects which estrange thee from thyself.

Then, like to a man awaking from a profound sleep, thou wilt open thine eyes, and amazement will take hold of thy soul, because the abyss towards which thou art hastening reveals itself to thee.

And if I cease not to strike, after having enlightened thy spirit by My divine light, it is that I may consummate the expiation of evil; for thou knowest it is written: "The moment of tribulation is that of recompence."

O, My son! let thy heart not revolt against suffering. For is it not in My hands as the instrument by which I try thy virtue?

Thou sayest: "Lord, Lord, what shall separate me from Thee? Shall it be affliction, or displeasure, or hunger, or nakedness, or the words of men, or persecution, or the sword?"

And thou sayest: "I am assured that neither principalities, or powers, or things present, or future, or violence, or all that which is most exalted, or most profound, or any earthly creature, can ever separate me from the love of my God."

And it is because thou sayest these things, that I make affliction weigh heavily on thee, that so thou mayest render Me this testimony, not alone by the words that issue from thy lips, but by the actions of thy will.

And if I try thy virtue by sufferings, is it not by these same that I purify it?

Howsoever just thou mayest be, dost thou not still fall seven times in the day? and do not My eyes distinguish in thy soul blemishes that thine own perception cannot discover?

When compared to God, can man be justified? and he who is born of woman, can he be pure?

For, behold, in My presence the moon herself is not resplendent, nor are the very stars without blemish, and how much less so shall be man, who is nothing more than a worm?

There is within thy soul a spirit of resistance which tarnishes her lustre, even as the lightest breath dims the fairest mirror.

And this resistance forms above her, as it were, a subtle vapour, which arrests the rays of light I would fain diffuse into her bosom with plenitude.

Now do I say unto thee in truth, as the mists which, soaring into the heavens, are chased away by the wind, even so those clouds which ravish from thy soul the plenitude of My light are dissipated by suffering.

And if thus it be, how mayest thou still give utterance to this complaint in the hour of affliction: "Perish the day on which I was born, and the hour in which a man was formed."

Others, again, say: "We refuse not the labour of suffering, but wherefore has not the choice of the trial been placed in our hands?"

And these, raising their voices, exclaim: "Lord, Lord, maintain the substance of Thy actions, but let the circumstances depend on our will.

"Thou hast permitted that we should be humbled to excess; but this humiliation, wherefore should it proceed from those whom we have most loved?

"We will those things which Thou dost will, but we will them differently. It has pleased Thee to afflict us, but wherefore does not this affliction end with the setting of the sun?"

Truly, do I tell thee, beware of imitating those who hold this language.

He who unites his will to Mine in suffering, accepts the trial after the manner in which I send it. He knows how much I abhor all rapine in the holocaust, and his heart makes no reserve.

O, My son! do I not know better than thou dost that which is suitable for thee?

I know that which is fitting for the parched up soil; and behold how I press between My hands the clouds of heaven, so as to draw forth those waters that shall quench its thirst.

I know that which is expedient to give to each

species of animal in order to sustain its existence; and, behold, how I make the grass of the fields grow for the one, whilst to the other I send its fleshy prey, that its hunger may be sated.

I know how they should be clad in the time of chilling frost, and, behold I draw from their substance the fleecy covering that preserves them from the rigours of the wintry wind.

I know what manner of nutriment and of beverage is needful for thy body; and, behold, why I ripen the ears of corn, and spread out the branches of the vine.

And, now, as knowing that which is suited to the earth, to the animals of all species, and to thy body, how should I not likewise know that affliction which is most salutary for thy soul?

And do I not know thy soul as intimately as I do the entrails of the earth?

And do I penetrate into her less than I do into thy organs, and the organs of the various animals I have created for thy service?

Thy sight is short, and thence it happens that the affliction which thou deemest hurtful, is, in effect, advantageous; and the tribulation which thou judgest salutary would become pernicious.

But, for Me, I know thy inclinations and thy wants, thy weaknesses and thy misery, and I ordain all things in consequence of this knowledge.

Say not then: " Wherefore, Lord, are Thy arrows fixed in me, wherefore does their sharpness parch up my spirit, wherefore do Thy terrors combat against me?

"Wherefore dost Thou bestow Thy light on a miserable being? and wherefore dost Thou give existence to him who awaits death with the impatience of those who dig into the earth in expectation of that treasure which they cannot attain?

"What force have I got that may bear me up? My force is not as that of the stones, and my flesh is not as bronze."

Neither say thou: "Lord, Lord, change this sorrow into that other; change this chalice of bitterness into another."

Receive with submission the suffering which visits thee, as likewise the manner of the visitation; and so thou wilt have perfected the union of thy will with Mine.

Happy he who receives all sorrow and all sadness in this manner; for he may say in truth: "Lord, Lord, Thou knowest that I love Thee."

V.

The Disciple.—O Master! be Thou blessed, because Thou hast shown me the way that leads to that union which Thy doctrines have made my heart desire.

Be Thou blessed for that sanction Thou hast

given to Thy commandments, for those joys and those sorrows which Thou pourest into my soul, like unto a salutary balm over a gaping wound.

The words Thou hast pronounced to me have fixed my spirit on that place where Thy will doth abide, and lo! I have said: "Lord, give me the wings of the dove, and I shall flee to that place, that I may repose therein."

The Master.—Truly, till this day I have taught thee by My words to unite thy will to Mine, but it is needful that I should now press thee, by My example, to consummate this union.

In the head of the book it was written of Me, that I shall do the will of My Father, and behold I came into the world, saying:

"O My Father! Thou hast not been content with such holocausts as have been offered to Thee heretofore; they were not worthy of Thee, but in bestowing on Me this body Thou hast rendered Me capable of honouring Thee by My obedience, and I have said: 'I come.'"

And now, that which I had said, have I not done it, and My sustenance, has it not been to accomplish unceasingly the will of Him who had sent Me?

O My son! behold and contemplate this mystery. I enter into the world, and that entrance is the first act by which I unite My will to that of My Father.

I descend from the eternal hills, because I obey Him who so loved the world that He gave for its salvation His only Son.

And this same obedience, which commences with My existence, extends to all the circumstances of My life, with that same plenitude with which My power extends over all My works.

My Father had inspired the Prophets, and the Prophets had spoken.

And the first had said: "Seventy weeks are shortened upon my people, and upon Thy holy city, that transgression may be finished, and sin may have an end, and iniquity may be abolished, and everlasting justice may be brought, and vision and prophecy may be fulfilled, and the Saint of saints may be anointed.

"Know thou, therefore, and take notice, that from the going forth of the word, to build up Jerusalem again unto Christ the Prince, there shall be seven weeks and sixty-two weeks."

And did I not come after the seven weeks, and the sixty-two weeks, as My Father willed, on that day when He set these words of prediction on the lips of the Prophet?

And then another had said: "And there shall come forth a rod out of the root of Jesse, and a flower shall rise out of his root, and the Spirit of the Lord shall rest upon him."

And again, others had said: "Behold the Lord God will come with strength, and His arm shall rule; behold His reward is with Him, and His work is before Him.

"He shall judge the poor with justice, and shall reprove with equity for the meek of the earth."

Again, another had said: "Thou, Bethlehem Ephrata, art a little one among the thousands of Juda; out of thee shall He come forth unto Me, that is to be the ruler of Israel."

And did I not choose, in conformity with the will of My Father, both the city and the tribe of My birth?

Did I not take for house and posterity the house and the posterity of David?

And yet another had said: "He shall grow up as a tender plant before Him, and as a root out of a thirsty ground. There is no beauty in Him, nor comeliness; and we have seen Him, and there was no sightliness that we should be desirous of Him.

"Thus saith the Lord, the Redeemer of Israel, His holy One, to the soul that is despised, to the nation that is abhorred, to the servant of rulers: Kings shall see, and princes shall rise up and adore for the Lord's sake."

And My will, did it not conform itself to that of My Father, contained in the words of the Prophet?

The obscurity and the poverty of My condition, did they not inspire with contempt those who encountered Me? When I arrived in some place, they retired, exclaiming: "Is not this the Son of the carpenter? Is this not the Son of Mary?"

And other prophets had said: "Justice shall be the girdle of His loins, and faith the girdle of His reins.

"He shall feed His flock like a shepherd, He

shall gather together the lambs with His arms, and He shall take them in His bosom.

"Behold thy King will come to thee, the Just and the Saviour; He is poor, and riding upon an ass.

"He shall not cry, nor have respect to persons; neither shall His voice be heard abroad."

And did I not appear conformably to the will of My Father, in justice and in fidelity, feeding My flock, and gathering together the lambs within My arms?

And yet another had said: "The eyes of the blind shall be opened, and the ears of the deaf shall be unstopped; then shall the lame leap as a hart, and the tongue of the dumb shall be free."

And knowest thou not that I have spoken, and that by the power of My word the blind recovered their sight, and the lame walked, and the deaf heard, and the lepers were healed?

And another had said: "*Despised and the most abject of men, a man of sorrows acquainted with infirmity......whereupon we esteemed Him not.*

"*Surely He hath borne our infirmity, and carried our sorrows, and we have thought Him as it were a leper.*

"*He was wounded for our iniquities, He was bruised for our sins, and the chastisement of our peace was upon Him.*"

And another had said: "*Awake, O sword, against My Shepherd, and against the man that cleaveth to Me, saith the Lord of Hosts; strike the shepherd and the sheep shall be scattered.*

"*And I will pour out upon the house of David, and upon the inhabitants of Jerusalem, the spirit of grace and of prayers, and they shall look upon Me whom they shall have pierced, and they shall mourn for Him.*"

And have I not submitted to all these sufferings, to all these humiliations? Is there one only desire of My Father, proclaimed through the mouth of the prophets, which I have not accomplished?

Open the book, and therein thou shalt find that which is written: "Christ has shown Himself obedient unto death, even to the death of the cross."

My son, listen yet to Me. I obeyed the will of My Father, and My obedience was not sullied by the voice of culpable revolt.

It remained perfect in joy as in sadness, in glory as in humiliation and opprobrium.

The will of My Father was evinced in this, that He permitted men to accuse Me, and to overwhelm Me with confusion by the words they uttered against Me.

It was declared in the power He granted them, to lay on Me their sacrilegious hands.

And when these men accused Me, and when they touched Me, I held My peace as a little child that knows not how to speak.

Hadst thou penetrated the depths of that sorrowful night, that covered Me with its shadows on the heights of Gethsemani, behold that which thou shouldst have seen.

Thou shouldst have seen the Son of Man betrayed by one of His disciples, and all those who had followed Him disperse and abandon Him.

Thou shouldst have beheld the Son of Man conducted to the mansion of the High-priest, and they who held Him ridiculed Him and struck Him.

They bandaged His eyes, they smote Him on the face, they questioned Him, saying: "Prophecy unto us, who is he who struck Thee?"

Thou listenedst, and the Son of Man was silent. Thou beheldest two false witnesses enter the assembly of His enemies, and those false witnesses said: "This Man has said, I am able to destroy the temple of God, and after three days to rebuild it;" and thou didst see the High-priest rise from his seat, exclaiming: "Answerest Thou nothing to the things which these witness against Thee." Thou didst listen, and the Son of Man was silent.

Thou didst see the High-priest rise the second time from his seat, crying out: "I adjure Thee, by the living God, to tell me if Thou be the Christ, the Son of God."

Thou didst hear the Son of Man answer in these words: "Thou hast said it."

Thou beheldest the High-priest, as he heard those words, rend his garments; thou didst hear him exclaim: "He has blasphemed, what further need have we of witnesses; what think you?" And they answered: "He is worthy of death."

Thou didst listen, and the Son of Man was silent.

Thou beheldest from the break of day how the princes of the priests, and the senators of the people, held council, and led the Son of Man into the presence of the governor, and the governor questioning Him, said to Him: "Dost Thou not hear how great testimonies they allege against Thee?"

Thou didst listen, and the Son of Man held His peace.

Hear still on.

I obeyed the will of My Father, and My obedience was eager.

Before the hour assigned for the consummation of the sacrifice, didst thou not see My breast swell as does the breast of him who falls into anguish through the ardour of his desires?

Thou didst hear My voice, and that voice exclaimed: "I am in suffering, My soul is in constraint till the hour when all shall be consummated."

In that night of woe, when thou didst follow Me, behold that which thou didst witness.

Thou beheldest the Son of Man sitting down to table with His disciples, and showing them shortly afterwards that one amongst them who was to betray Him.

And thou didst behold the perfidious disciple

retire before the end of supper, as he went out to execute his guilty project.

Thou listenedst, and the Son of Man said to the traitor: "That which thou wilt do, do it quickly."

Thou didst behold the Son of Man ascend the mountain of Olives, and remain there for some time apart.

Thou beheldest Him turn the eyes of His soul towards His Father, return twice successively to His disciples in order to awake them from their slumber.

Thou beheldest Him come for the third time; thou listenedst, and the Son of Man pronounced these words: "Behold the hour is at hand when I shall be delivered into the hands of sinners. He who will betray Me is nigh. Rise, let us go."

Thou didst behold the Son of Man betrayed with a kiss, and armed men surround Him on all sides, so as to lay hands on Him.

Thou beheldest the disciple who loved Him draw his sword to defend Him, and cut off the right ear of one of the armed men, who was the servant of the High-priest.

Thou heardest, and the Son of Man said to the disciple:

"Thinkest thou that I cannot ask My Father, and He will give Me presently more than twelve legions of angels?

"Why should I not drink of the chalice My Father has given Me? How, then, shall the Scriptures be fulfilled, that so it must be done?"

Thou didst hearken to the words of the Son of Man, when He said to the disciple:

"Peter, put up thy sword into its place, for all that take the sword shall perish with the sword."

Hear on still farther.

I obeyed the will of My Father, and My obedience was not as that of the captive led by the hand of his brothers to a cruel torment.

My obedience was joyous; I beheld My cross from the eternal days, and I drew nigh to it with love.

And that which man performs with love, how should he not accomplish it with great joy?

The spouse who seeks his beloved can weep and feel sadness in the depths of his heart before he has found her.

And yet, there is in his tears and in his sadness, a profound joy, for he exclaims: "How beautiful art thou, my beloved! Thou hast wounded my heart with one of thy eyes, and with one hair of thy neck.

"Thy lips are as a dropping honey-comb; honey and milk are under thy tongue, and the smell of thy garments as the smell of frankincense.

"For winter is now past, the rain is over and gone. Arise, My beloved, and come."

And have I not sought My cross as the spouse seeks his beloved?

Before I found her, I wept, and My soul was sad unto death, but My heart beat in her presence with a joy that was infinite and divine.

The joy of a man who has found a treasure, compared to that supreme satisfaction should grow pallid, like to a feeble light in the brightness of the noon-day.

I beheld the chalice of bitterness that the will of My Father had prepared and placed on My way.

I saw it from the eternal days, and I took that chalice, and said: "How fair is this chalice! Its wine doth penetrate and inebriate Me."

O My son! it is because I obeyed without murmuring, and with an ineffable eagerness, and with an infinite joy, that I formed between My humanity and the divine essence of My Father an intimate and an eternal union.

And lo! how I might say in truth: My Father and I are but one; all that which He possesses is Mine, all that which I possess is His.

Happy he who will follow Me in the ways of obedience, for to him is it given to say: "Lord, by my fidelity to Thy commandments I will that which Thou willest, and in thus willing I have dilated my heart."

SECOND COLLOQUY.

THE DISCIPLE DEMANDS BY WHAT MEANS HE MAY ARRIVE AT THE LOVE OF HEAVENLY THINGS, AT SACRIFICE AND UNION.—THE MASTER REPLIES THAT HE MUST PRAY.—THE DISCIPLE COMPLAINS; HE HAS PRAYED ACCORDING TO HIS OWN WILL, AND WITHOUT UNITING HIMSELF TO THE WILL OF HIS MASTER.—THE MASTER INSTRUCTS HIM IN WHAT MANNER HE SHOULD PRAY.

SECOND COLLOQUY.

I.

The Disciple.—I know that Thou hast accomplished all those things announced by the lips of Thy prophets.

Thou hast said: "O Father! not My will but Thy will be done!"

And, moreover, Thou hast said: "O Father! that which is to be, let it not happen after the manner I will, but let it be as Thou dost will."

Thou hast said: "O, Father! I do with joy all that which Thou hast ordained, because it is pleasing in Thine eyes that I should thus act."

And because Thou hast done as Thou hast said, Thou hast rendered testimony before men to that unity which exists betwixt Thy heavenly Father and Thee.

O, Master! how shall I follow Thee? shall not some divine pulsation pass from Thy heart into mine, which may strengthen it in this way of obedience which conducts to perfect union, to increasing love?

And if I speak as Thou hast spoken, if I say: "O, Master! let not my will, but Thine, be done," may I not then hope to accomplish my promise?

The Master.—In truth, all that is impossible to man, but to God all things are possible.

My son, thou must pray, this is My commandment; and, if thou observest it not, hope not to be enabled to speak as I have spoken, or to be faithful to thy word.

He who is placed in dependence, has he not need to implore in his misery him on whom he depends?

And art thou not under the dependence of thy celestial Father? and in His sight art thou not as a mendicant who awaits on the wayside the passage of the rich man?

Amongst the sons of men, is there one alone who can, without Him, count on one single moment?

Thy destinies, are they placed in thy hands? and canst thou add a single inch to thy stature, or canst thou render one hair of thine head either white or black?

Thou sowest and thou plantest, but if thy celestial Father did not give the increase, should not the sweat of thy brow be poured out for nothing?

And if in things material thou dost so depend, what shall be thy dependence in those of the spirit?

Hast thou not read that which is written: "Without Me thou canst do nothing." If left alone, how canst thou unite thy will to Mine?

Can the sons of men have one good thought by themselves?

This power, must it not be the gift of My Father? Must they not strive against flesh and blood, against the principalities and the powers of hell, against the rulers of this world of darkness, and against the spirits of wickedness in the high places?

O, My son! thou art poor and dependent, and therefore have I said to thee: "Thou must pray."

Help and abundance dwell in the high places; raise thy soul to the throne of grace; ask, and thou shalt receive; knock, and it shall opened unto thee. Thou seekest to unite thy will to Mine; now, I say unto thee in truth, the germ of that union is to be found in prayer.

The act of thanksgiving that comes from the heart, does it not respond to that action of love which visits thee from on high with the heavenly gift?

And wherefore then should this germ remain undeveloped? Does the celestial Father deny to the plants the dews and the rays of the sun which may give them increase?

Truly, truly, I say to thee, all that which thou wilt ask of My Father in My name, He will grant it thee.

Thou wilt invoke Him, and He shall hear thee; thou wilt call Him, and He will answer thee: "Here I am."

Even before thou wilt raise thy voice, thou shalt be heard; and before thou wilt have ceased speaking, He shall have granted thy prayer.

In virtue of that power by which He speaks

within thee, He can do infinitely more than all thou canst ask of Him, than all thou canst think.

Thou art poor, and in thy poverty thou desirest the riches of that grace which conduces to union, and which constitutes union itself.

Let thy heart be not agitated or disquieted. Pray, for thou knowest that thy Heavenly Lord hearkens to the desire of the poor, and that His ear is attentive to the dispositions of their hearts.

It was by prayer that Moses resisted the multitude of the enemies' forces, and that he saved the people of Israel in the battle.

It was through prayer that this great servant of God obtained grace for his guilty people.

"See," saith the Lord, to Moses, "see, that this people is stiff-necked.

"Let Me alone, that My wrath may be kindled up against them, and that I may destroy them. And I will make of thee the chief of a great nation."

And the prophet said: "Why, O Lord, is Thy indignation enkindled against Thy people, whom Thou hast brought out of the land of Egypt with great power, and with a mighty hand?"

And the prophet continued: "Remember Abraham and Isaac and Israel, Thy servants, to whom Thou sworest by Thy own self, saying: I will multiply your seed as the stars of heaven.

"Let Thy anger cease, and be appeased upon the wickedness of Thy people."

And the Lord was appeased, and He no longer

willed to exterminate this nation, as He had meant to do.

It was by prayer that another prophet tamed the fury of lions, and that three youths cast into the furnace came forth without feeling in their flesh the ardour of the devouring flames.

It was by means of prayer that a mother afflicted with sterility became fruitful, and that an illustrious prophet was born.

It was by prayer that a king according to God's own heart obtained victories, and that Ezechias made the war to cease without having recourse to the strength of arms or the din of trumpets.

Open the book, and read that which is written: They wandered in the parched and barren desert, without being enabled to find the way leading to the destined city. They suffered hunger and thirst to exhaustion.

But, having had recourse to the Lord in this extremity, He delivered them from the necessity to which they were reduced, He placed them in the true way leading to the destined city.

They languished in gloomy prisons, charged with irons, sunk in the most abject indigence, and awaiting the stroke of death.

They turned to their heavenly Lord in their extremities, and He delivered them from their misery.

He broke their chains, He rescued them from their gloomy dungeons.

They were crushed by the maladies to which their iniquities had conducted them; they had in abhorrence all species of nutriment, and they were nigh to the gates of death.

They had recourse to the Almighty Lord in these extremities, and He delivered them, His divine will healed them, and rescued them from death.

Behold those men, now borne aloft with their barks into the very heavens, anon dashed downwards into the depths below, and withering with dread at the sight of the evils which menace them.

Troubled and tottering, as though intoxicated, they find no succour within themselves against the violence of the tempest.

They turn to the Almighty Lord, and, lo! He delivers them from the danger. He changes the fury of the tempest into a gale mild and genial, and He stills the voice of the billows.

I say unto thee truly, My Father hears every prayer; wherefore, then, shouldst thou not feel arising within thy heart the confidence of observing thy promise?

There are some who say: "O Lord, deliver us from the fury of lions, and let these beasts become as lambs at our sides," and these men are heard.

And he who prays to obtain love in these terms: "O, Master, do Thou render me faithful to Thine ordinances, which are full of justice;" how may this man not be heard?

Others say: "O Lord, let these burning flames not consume our bodies, but let them act on our flesh as a refreshment." And these men are likewise heard.

And he who petitions for love in these terms: "O, Master, I would fain do joyfully that which is agreeable to Thine eyes;" how may this man not be heard?

There are others who say: "Lord, do Thou break our chains, do Thou rescue us from the hands of our enemies, and deliver us from these dismal prisons." And these men are heard.

And he who solicits for love in these words: "O, Master! let that which is to be, not happen after the manner I will, but as Thou willest;" how should he not be heard?

Others, again, say: "Take compassion on the work of Thy hands, behold how we suffer hunger and thirst, even to exhaustion, and are already at the gates of death;" and the prayer of these men is heard.

And he who solicits love in these words: "O, Master! let not my will, but Thine, be done;" how should he not be heard?

My son, listen to Me, and learn of Me that thou must pray at all times.

The hour was nigh when I was to preach to the poor of the earth, and accomplish in all respects the will of My Father, and if thou didst follow Me from that hour, behold that which thou didst see.

Thou beheldest the Son of Man issue from the waves of the Jordan, and repair to the desert to be tempted by the wicked spirit; and thou be-

beheldest this evil one accost Him, saying unto Him: "If Thou be the Son of God, command these stones to be made bread.

"And the evil spirit took Him into the holy city, and set Him upon a pinnacle of the temple, and spoke to Him thus: If Thou be the Son of God, cast Thyself down, for it is written: He has given His angels charge over Thee.

"Again the wicked spirit took Him up into a very high mountain, from whence He saw in one instant all the kingdoms of the earth, and said unto Him: All these I will give Thee, if Thou wilt fall down and adore me."

Thou listenedst, and the Son of Man answered and prayed.

Thou beheldest the Son of Man call His disciples to Him, select twelve from amongst them, in order to send them to preach the Gospel, and grant them the power of healing the sick, and of chasing away the spirits of darkness.

And thou beheldest the Son of Man on the eve of that day on which He chose the twelve, thou beheldest Him retire to the mountain and there pass the night.

Thou didst listen, and the Son of Man prostrated Himself and prayed.

Thou beheldest Him as He preached the Gospel to the poor, and as He made the blind to see, the deaf to hear, the dumb to speak; and when at the evening hour He retired once more to the mountain, and there passed the night, thou didst bend thine ear, and the Son of Man prostrated Himself, and prayed.

Thou beheldest Him one day turn to His disciples, saying to them these words: "Behold the time cometh, and is already, when you shall be dispersed, and you shall leave Me alone.

"Much suffering awaits you in the world, but take courage, I have vanquished the world."

Then, after He had ceased to speak, thou listenedst again, and the Son of Man prostrated Himself, and prayed.

He raised His eyes to heaven, and said: "O, Father! the hour is come, glorify Thy Son.

"Now glorify Thou Me with Thyself, with the glory which I had with Thee before the world was."

And, raising His eyes towards heaven, He said again: "O Father, I pray for them whom Thou hast given Me, because they are Thine.

"Holy Father, keep them in Thy name whom Thou hast given Me, that they may be one as We also are.

"I pray not that Thou shouldst take them out of the world, but that Thou shouldst keep them from evil.

"Sanctify them in truth, Thy word is truth.

"And not for them only do I pray, but for them also who through Thy word shall believe in Me, that they all may be one, as Thou, Father, in Me, and as I in Thee.

"I in them, and Thou in Me, that they may be made perfect in one, and the world may know that Thou hast sent Me, and hast loved them as Thou hast also loved Me."

And the Son of Man still prayed, and He said: "Father! I will that where I am they also whom Thou hast given Me may be with Me, that so they may see My glory which Thou hast given Me, because Thou hast loved Me before the creation of the world."

Thou didst see the Son of Man one day repair to a town called Bethania, and on His arrival, a woman cast herself at His feet, saying to Him: "Lord, if Thou hadst been here, my brother should not have died."

And thou didst see the Son of Man weep, and go to the place of sepulture.

And before thou heardest these words, "Lazarus, come forth," what didst thou hear?

Thou listenedst, and the Son of Man raised His voice, and prayed: "O Father," said He, "I give Thee thanks that Thou hast heard Me."

Thou didst see the Son of Man towards evening time ascend the mountain of Olives, remove to a distance from His disciples, and await the coming of His hour.

Thou didst see Him begin to fear and to be full of sadness.

Thou didst bend thine ear, and the Son of Man prostrated Himself in prayer.

"O, Father!" said He, "let this chalice pass away from Me, yet let Thy will, and not Mine, be done."

At the third hour of the day, thou didst see

the Son of Man abandon both hands and feet to His executioners, in order to be crucified.

Thou didst see Him raised from the earth that this word might be fulfilled: And if I be lifted up from the earth, I shall draw all things to Myself.

Thou didst bend thine ear, and the Son of Man raised His eyes to heaven and prayed.

"O, Father, forgive them," said He, "for they know not what they do."

Thou didst hear the Son of Man when He cried out at the ninth hour of the day: "My God, My God, why hast Thou forsaken Me?"

Thou didst behold Him as He cast a last look, as it were, to see if there were nothing wanting to the sacrifice, and as He cried out with a strong voice: "All is consummated."

Thou listenedst once again, and the Son of Man lifted His eyes for the last time towards heaven, and prayed. "Father," He exclaimed, "into Thy hands I commend My spirit."

O My son! the plenitude of the Divinity resides in Me, for I am the Word, and thou knowest that it is written that in the beginning was the Word, and the Word was God.

And, nevertheless, I prayed.

All treasures of the wisdom and of the knowledge of God are contained in My person; for all that which the Father possesses, the Son likewise possesses.

All power was given Me in heaven and on earth; for the power of the Father is the power of the Son.

And yet I prayed.

O thou who seekest for love, follow My ways, for I say unto thee truly, he who prays commences to love, and when his prayer is ended all is perfect union and increasing love.

II.

The Disciple.—O Master, I prayed, and my will was not detached from itself to unite itself to Thine. I prayed, and my heart was not visited by love. Is Thy word, then, vain?

Wouldst Thou have deceived the children of men in saying to them: "Ask, and you shall receive, knock, and it shall be opened unto you"?

O, Master! I know that Thy word is truth, I know likewise that I have prayed, and that I have not been heard. Do Thou expound to me this mystery.

The Master.—My son, learn from Me how thou must pray, and the desires of thy heart shall not perish.

Before thou prayest, do thou prepare thy soul, and beware of being like to a man who would tempt God.

Acknowledge thy misery and thy meanness, humble thyself at the sight of thy iniquities, and let thy plaint be unceasing; for it is written: "The Lord resists the proud, but He gives His grace to the humble."

The prayer of him who humbles himself pierces the clouds, it shall not be satisfied till it shall have reached the throne of God, and it shall not withdraw from the presence of the Most High without being heard.

He whose sanctuary is in the heights of the heavens, abides likewise in hearts contrite and humble, for they are more pleasing in His eyes than are the most magnificent of temples.

Heaven is His mansion, the earth is His footstool; what dwelling wilt thou build for Him, and on what spot hast thou fixed for His resting-place?

It is His hand which has created all these things, and they are, because He has made them.

But on whom will He cast His eyes, if not on the poor man, whose heart within him is broken, and who hears His words with fear?

Does the indigent man draw nigh to the rich with arrogance? In his desire to obtain his demand, he bows his head, and seeks not to sustain the glance of him who is stronger than himself.

And art thou not, in the presence of thy Father, as the deepest misery which draws nigh to the greatest opulence?

Prepare thy soul, as does the mendicant his countenance, and the Lord will hearken to thy prayer, and He will not disdain thy supplications.

He will shed down on thee His grace as a fertile dew, for He is nigh to those who groan, and He saves the humble of spirit.

Listen, and comprehend once more the word I have spoken: "All those things which thou demandest in prayer with confidence, thou shalt obtain."

Without faith there is no prayer, for how can men invoke Him in whom they do not believe?

Truly, I say unto thee, beware of doubting when thou prayest, for he who is wanting in confidence is like to the waves of the ocean, borne away and shaken by the wind.

Open the book, and read that which is written.

It was through prayer that a barren woman received the boon of fertility, when she was already stricken in years.

It was through that means that from one man alone, who was as it were dead, there arose a posterity as numerous as the stars in the heavens, as the grains of sand in the sea.

It was by faith that the people of Israel passed over the Red Sea as on the dry ground, whilst the Egyptians, wishing to try the same passage, were swallowed up in the waves.

It was by faith that men according to God's own heart conquered kingdoms, fulfilled the obligations of justice, and reaped the reward of the promise.

It was by faith that they arrested the violence of the flames, that they escaped the edge of the sword, that they became cured of their maladies, and were filled with strength and courage in the fight.

There are some who say: "Lord, grant us

those goods we ask of Thee;" and in so saying they believe that the Lord does not hear them, and they open not their hearts to confidence.

Others again, say: "Lord, deliver us from those evils that crush us;" and in so saying they cast their eyes on their own weakness and misery, and believe themselves unworthy of being heard.

My son, do thou beware of imitating these men, who pray and yet fear to remain unheard, and who fix their eyes on their iniquities, as though it were to destroy all feeling of confidence.

The celestial Father hears the least plaint of His creatures, and ever responds to it according to His mercy, and not according to His justice.

Hast thou not read that which is written: "Lord, Thou wilt pardon my sin, for it is grievous."

The poor man who asks, does he not place his confidence in his own misery and abjection?

And, less wretched, he hopes the less; more afflicted, he hopes the more.

And, if the heart of the rich be touched, is it not the misery of this unfortunate which has moved it?

Have confidence, therefore, when thou dost pray. Thy misery, is it not immeasurable? and thy abjection, is it not deeper than the abysses?

I say to thee, in truth, have confidence, for thou dost say, in imploring the rich man: My father, and the heart of this thy heavenly Father is always moved.

He is moved for the flowers of the fields; the

lilies of the waste demand of Him to be clothed, and He clothes them with more splendour than was arrayed Solomon in the height of his glory.

He is moved for the least amongst the little sparrows, two of which are not worth above a groat. They cry to Him, and not one of them falls to the ground without His permission.

How, then, should He not be touched by thy prayer, when thou invokest Him with confidence?

If He be the Father of the rains and of the dewdrops, and of the lilies of the field, and of the smallest sparrow, is He not likewise thy Father, and in a manner more sublime and more perfect?

Has He not voluntarily engendered thee by the word of His truth, and art thou not become by faith and by grace a child born, not of blood, nor of the will of the flesh, nor of that of man, but of God Himself?

Is it not He who has conferred on thee the spirit of adoption and of love, which prays within thee, and through which thou dost cry: "My Father! my Father!"

Till now, thou hast but too much compared thy celestial Father with the children of men, to whom are addressed supplications which are unheard in the hardness of their hearts.

And, behold, why thou hast not demanded love with the confidence of obtaining it; and, as not having thus solicited, thou hast not obtained it.

But, lo! the hour approaches when thou shalt comprehend this word: "They have tempted the

Lord in saying: Is God amongst us, or is He not?"

And when that hour shall come, thy heart will say: "O, Master! I have believed, and therefore have I spoken."

My son, listen on, and learn from Me how thou shouldst pray.

If thou didst follow the Son of Man, thou wouldst have seen Him one day bend His steps to the well of Jacob, accost a woman of Samaria, speaking to her these words: "The hour cometh, and now is, when the true adorers shall adore the Father in spirit and in truth, for the Father also seeketh such to adore Him.

"God is a Spirit, and they that adore Him must adore Him in spirit and in truth."

O, thou! who seekest for love, do thou pray thus.

What avails it, if whilst thy lips move, thy heart be far from Me?

That which My Father expects in order to conform to thy desires, is that thy heart should speak to Him, that thine eyes should seek Him.

Till now, thou hast uttered words; the air has been beaten by the echo of thy voice; but My Father has touched with His hand these words and these sounds.

And, touching them, He found them colder than the ice that covers the waters in the season of the biting frost.

The breath of the heart, which is like to the wind of the south, had not penetrated and given them life; and, behold, why they have not called down upon thee the spirit of charity and love.

When thou prayest, affect not to speak much, as do the heathens, who imagine they will obtain by dint of words.

Do thou beware of resembling these, for thy Father knows thy wants, even before thou dost utter thy prayer.

Presume not on thine own force, for many of those who speak much, pray not in spirit and in truth.

They commence with ardour, but fatigue gains on them, and, the angel of prayer, who transmits all petitions, hears but a murmur, like unto those confused voices that are heard in the distance.

When thou prayest be not like these hypocrites, who affect to pray in the synagogue and at the corners of the streets, but with a view to be remarked.

Truly, truly, do I say unto thee: "These have already received their reward."

Thou, on the contrary, when thou wouldst pray, enter thy chamber, and make fast the door, then pray to thy Father in secret, and He who reads into the depths of thy heart will reward thee.

He who prays with a view to be seen by men, how can he pray in spirit and in truth?

For does not his pride become as a raging fire, which consumes his supplications, and destroys within him all germ of virtue?

I have said: "Ask, and you shall receive;

seek, and you shall find; knock, and it shall be opened unto thee."

He who asks shall receive, he who seeks shall find, and whosoever knocks, it shall be opened unto him.

And he who prays in order to be seen by men, speaks, but he demands not; he comes forth from his repose, but he seeks not; he raises his hands, yet he does not knock.

Therefore, abandon external things, retire within thyself, and make of thy soul a solitude, for it is written: "He whom I love, I shall conduct into solitude, and I shall speak to his heart."

Thy heavenly Father wills the sacrifice of the lips, and the offering of thanksgiving, but He wills not that this sacrifice should be as are those dried bones that lie in the depths of the sepulchres.

Consequently, let thy words be vivified by the ardour of the soul, and thy words shall be prayer, and prayer shall become grace.

My son, hear Me on: thou desirest the union of thy will to Mine; thou desirest love: do thou ask of My Father this union and this love in My name, and He will grant them thee.

Salvation is effected through love, and thou knowest that it is written: "There is no other name save Mine in virtue of which thou canst be saved."

Through Me alone thou canst go to My Father, for I am the way, the truth, and the life.

Till now, thou hast not prayed in My name,

and thou hast obtained nothing; do thou pray in My name, and thou shalt receive.

Pray anew, and without ceasing, for I have said: "We must always pray, and never grow weary."

There are in the treasures of mercy days of trial for the children of men.

They rise at the break of day, they pray a first time, and it would seem to them as though they were not heard.

During the day time, they pray again a second time, then a third time, and it would still appear to them as though they were not heard.

Already the sun declines, and his fires are less ardent; but truly do I say unto thee, his last ray will not have disappeared till perfect joy shall have been shed down on their hearts.

Didst thou follow the Son of Man on the road to Tyre and Sidon, behold that which thou didst see.

Thou didst behold a woman approach Him, and that woman exclaimed: "Lord Jesus, Son of David, have mercy on me, for my daughter is grievously tempted by a devil."

Thou didst listen, and the Son of Man answered not. Thou heardest that woman exclaim a second time: "Lord Jesus, Son of David, have pity on me."

Thou didst listen, and the Son of Man said: "I was not sent but to the sheep that are lost of Israel." Thereupon, thou didst behold that woman prostrate herself at His feet, and adore

Him, crying aloud: "Lord, Lord, help me!" Thou heardest the Son of Man exclaim: "It is not good to take the bread of children and to cast it to the dogs. Let the children be first sated."

And thou heardest that woman exclaim: "Yea, Lord, for the whelps also eat of the crumbs that fall from the table of their masters."

Thou listenedst, and the Son of Man said: "O, woman! great is thy faith, be it done to thee as thou wilt." And the evil spirit departed from her daughter.

O thou who demandest love, remember that woman, and pray as she prayed.

When thou speakest to My Father in My name, and when thou hearest not His consoling voice, do thou speak once more.

Let not sadness fatigue thy heart, nor let discouragement penetrate into its sanctuary.

Thy words are counted, as are the hairs of thine head, and not one of them shall be left without its recompense.

Thou hast received the spirit of adoption, which makes thee cry out. Cease not then, to cry aloud, for it is written: "The Lord does justice to His elect, who cry to Him day and night."

The silence of My Father is ordained as a trial, but this trial passes away; and then it is given to hear that voice which chaunts: "My peace be with you."

THIRD COLLOQUY.

THE DISCIPLE DEMANDS IN WHAT MANNER IT IS FITTING TO LOVE SOULS AND LABOUR FOR THE ESTABLISHMENT OF HARMONY AMONGST THEM.—THE MASTER REPLIES THAT BEFORE ALL THINGS IT IS NEEDFUL TO PREPARE THE HEART.—HE TEACHES HIM NOT TO JUDGE, BECAUSE JUDGMENT DESTROYS LOVE.—HE TEACHES HIM NOT TO SPEAK AGAINST HIS BRETHREN, BECAUSE THE MALICIOUS WORD SEVERS BROTHER FROM BROTHER.

THIRD COLLOQUY.

I.

The Disciple.—O, my Master! I have turned to Thee, I have prayed, and Thou knowest that I love Thee, do Thou instruct me how to love that which is not Thee.

Teach me how I should love that which is not beauty in its essence, that which is not perfection, or not sanctity, or not love infinite.

It is then alone I can be, amidst this people of souls that Thou dost cherish, as a light, as a support, and as an invisible bond.

Then alone I shall become as a corner stone of that edifice which Thou hast founded in a celestial harmony, in bringing to this earth the sacred flames of Thy love. O Master, grant me this science of love!

The Master.—Be thou blessed for those words thou hast uttered, and return thanks to My Father, for he who loves Me listens to Me, and he who listens to Me learns how it is fitting to love souls.

O, My son! I have deeply loved men, and now,

I tell thee, thou must love them, even as I loved them.

There are some, who, desiring good, attach themselves to those who practice it, and withdraw from evil men, and these men believe they love.

There are others, again, who, desirous of good, speak with men of iniquity; but, seeing that they are not listened to, they cease to speak: and these likewise believe they love.

They are deceived, for to reduce love it is to annihilate it, and woe to him who has destroyed love within his soul; better for that man he had never been born.

And there are other men, who, desirous of good, show themselves severe; they seek to repress the excesses of several, by words offensive and steeped in gall: and these men believe that they love.

And there are still others, who, solicitous for good, pardon their brothers a first, and a second time, but afterwards grow weary of pardoning, and these believe they love.

They are deceived: to reduce love is to annihilate it, and woe to the man who has destroyed love within his soul, better for him he had never been born.

Truly, truly, do I say unto thee, he who loves abandons not the wicked, he speaks, he ceases not to speak, he pardons, and he is not weary of pardoning.

O, My son! place thine hand on My heart, and answer Me, it is not thus I have loved men.

The Disciple.—O, Master! Thy word troubles me, remorse rises to the heights of my soul, as the waves beaten by the tempest mount into the air, and I hear a voice of condemnation announcing to me: "Thou hast never loved."

O, Master! abandon not Thy servant in his distress, make straight his ways, and let Thy light dispel his darkness.

The Master.—My son, fear not thou, the truth is ever revealed to him who is desirous to know it, and love is ever granted to him who wishes to love.

A grievous wound has struck mankind, and that is moral evil, or sin; and behold why men will not pursue their course in harmony, as the spheres which I have placed in the heights of the heavens.

They will not unite, they will not aid each other mutually, for the pride of the spirit and the covetousness of the flesh have destroyed in them all strength of union with all germ of love.

Dost thou will that these men, who live in isolation and dispersion, should unite and second each other? then, do thou shake off thy sleep, and accept the task.

Stretch forth thy hand against all prevarication, that it may be abolished, that iniquity may be effaced, and that sin may be at an end. This work is Mine, but I will that it be likewise thine.

As My Father sent Me, in like manner do I send thee; do thou hasten, for the day declines, and the hour is nigh when thou shouldst render an account of thy mission.

This task is great, but be not daunted, for all is possible to him who is with Me, all is easy to him who loves.

My grace is all-powerful, and love is stronger than death.

The Disciple.—By what means may I abolish all prevarication, efface iniquity, and destroy sin amongst men?

Thou knowest, O Master! that my word is vain, that it passes as the wind that blows, and leaves not a trace behind it; and, moreover, do men hear the words of other men?

The Master.—My son, they shall hearken to thy voice. It is written: Before prayer, prepare thy soul; and I say unto thee, before thou speakest unto men, prepare thine heart.

He who prepares his heart, disengages it from all evil thoughts, for charity thinks no evil; judge not thy brothers, lest that love which thou shouldst give them be destroyed within thee to its very root.

Sin enters the heart of him who judges, for to My Father alone belongs judgment; and if I have the power to judge, it is that My Father has given Me that power.

Who art thou that judgest the servant of another, for does not this alone behove Him who is his Master?

And when thou judgest thy brother, and when

thou thinkest ill of him in thy heart, is it not the servant of another whom thou dost judge?

Is it thou who givest life to thy brother? Is it thou who withdrawest that life from him? Is it thou who givest him the air which he breathes, or the bread that sustains him?

Thou canst say unto him: "Do this thing and that other," and his members will bend to thy will, but his soul may rise up without sin against the justice of thine orders; for it is written: "Thou shalt adore the Lord thy God, and Him alone thou shalt serve."

Therefore, leave judgment to Him who possesses authority, full and perfect, to him who says to thee and to thy brothers: "Without Me you can do nought."

Consequently, leave judgment to Him, for in order to judge thou must judge like Him, or else thou must not judge.

Thy Father, who is in heaven, judges the children of men, and His judgments are just and equitable, and it is because He sees into the depths of their souls.

He penetrates them with His glance, with more force than the water penetrates the earth.

He reads within the mind of man the thoughts which arise, and which he completes, as likewise those which arise, and which he leaves incomplete.

He distinguishes in his heart the sentiments which pass away, as well as those that abide, because He sounds the heart and the loins.

He measures with His glance the force of the temptations that pursue him, both in the day time and the night, as likewise the extent of his good will.

He scans equally the culpability in the fall, and the glory in the triumph, as he who takes the line to measure an acre of ground.

Who art thou, to judge as thy celestial Father? What is the power of thine eyes? Thou canst distinguish nought save that which is apparent, and even that imperfectly.

The birds of prey that soar into the air discover the least insect that shelters itself beneath the blade of grass, and thou who tramplest on that herb, thou dost not discern it.

Thy sight is short, and thou confidest not in it, when thou seekest to discover from a distance those objects which are apparent to the senses.

How, then, canst thou have confidence in this internal perception of thy soul, which is yet more bounded than that of thy body? Are there not in constant agitation around thee myriads of thoughts and of sentiments like to a torrent of dust which the wind whirls about on the highway?

And these thoughts, these sentiments, canst thou distinguish them? Are they not for thy soul as though they were not?

In that soul which draws nigh to thine own with a severe deliberation, thou wouldst distinguish a certain harshness, and there was, in effect, but a celestial suavity.

In that other soul which seeks thine with precipitation, as a steed in full career, there seemed to thee a commencement of delirium, of wild impetuosity, whereas there was in reality an ineffable love.

Thou seest not, else thou discernest ill; consequently, leave judgment to Him whose glance penetrates into the abysses, and who possesses essentially the secret of searching into hearts.

Leave judgment to Him, for justice precedes His judgments, as the clouds of heaven precede the lightning flash which plays in the immensity of space.

When thou judgest, may thy judgments say to justice: "You are my father and my mother."

Thou thinkest evil of thy brother, and thou condemnest him in thy heart, for this reason, that thou art evil thyself.

It is not alone thy spirit that impels thee against him, it is likewise thy passion. If that did not enter into thy soul as a consuming flame, thy spirit would remain calm, and more peaceful than the lamb that yields to the shearer his first fleece.

It would distinguish the good without seeking to discover the evil, and that vision would satisfy its avidity as a refreshing fruit sates the wearied traveller who journeys from break of day on a dusty way.

O, My son! contemplate thy celestial Father, and behold how great is His solicitude that His judgments may be just and equitable.

A vapour of crime arises from the midst of many a guilty city, and that vapour ascends upwards to Him.

The inhabitants of these cities have but the appetites of the brute, they move as the worms, and they lie grovelling in the mire.

Within them there is nothing remaining of humanity, and their breast sounds hollow, for they have lost all dignity and honour.

Abandoned to the genius of baseness, they lie crushed beneath the most abject of tyrannies under the sun, they are now but as the dust of men.

The vapour of their crimes ascends—ascends incessantly, and yet thy celestial Father judges them not.

He has beheld these men with the wounds that rendered them like to a wreck, and to infected rags, but, because His hand had blessed them, He will wait still longer.

Before judging them He shall descend as one who cannot see from afar, and He will see yet a second time: I shall descend, and I shall see.

And it is when He shall have descended, and when He shall have touched with His finger all this flesh of ignominy, that He shall pronounce the last word of His judgment.

Therefore, leave the judgment of thy brothers to Him who looks a first and a second time, lest thy judgments should not be just and equitable.

Truly, do I say unto thee, leave judgment to Him. Do thou beware of confiding in thine own light, and of resembling the Scribes and Pharisees.

These judged Me, and I convinced them of sin.

One day, as I instructed the people, Pharisees and Doctors of the law came into the assembly, and My power was manifested in the cure of the sick.

Thereupon four men arrived, bearing on a couch a paralytic whom they sought to bring in and to lay before Me.

But not knowing where to set him down by reason of the crowd, they climbed to the roof, uncovered it, and lowering down the sick man with his bed, bore him into the midst of the assembly.

And, seeing their faith, I said to the paralytic: "My son, take courage, thy sins are forgiven thee."

And the Scribes and the Pharisees who were present, began to reason and to say within themselves: "How may this man hold this language? He blasphemes. Who can remit sin save God alone?"

And, knowing their thoughts by My own perception, I said to them: "Why judge you evil within your hearts? Which is it easier to say to a sick man: Thy sins are forgiven thee; or else: Arise and walk?

"But that you may know that the Son of Man has the power on earth of remitting sins, I shall work this prodigy."

And, turning to the paralytic, I said to him: "Arise, take up thy bed, and go into thy house."

Upon which that man rose up before them, he took up the bed on which he lay, and went away to his own house.

Another day, as I was at table in the house of a Levite, publicans and sinners, who were there in great number, placed themselves with Me and My disciples, for many of these people had followed Me.

And the Scribes and Pharisees, seeing that I eat with sinners and publicans, said to My disciples: "Whence comes it that your Master eats and drinks with publicans and sinners?"

This they said, because they judged evil of Me, in the depths of their hearts.

And, having listened to them, I said to them: "They that are in health need not a physician, but they that are ill."

Go you, and learn the signification of these words: "I will mercy, and not sacrifice; for I am come, not to call the just, but sinners."

And, as My word had confounded them, they continued to judge Me ill; and, having combined with the disciples of John, they came to Me, and said:

"Why do the disciples of John and of the Pharisees fast, but Thy disciples do not fast?"

And I answered them a second time: "Can the children of the marriage fast as long as the bridegroom is with them? As long as they have the bridegroom with them they cannot fast.

"But the days will come when the bridegroom shall be taken away from them, and then they shall fast."

And thus did I condemn those who thought ill of Me, in showing them the culpability of their judgments; therefore, do thou fear, and judge not ill of thy brother, for it is written: "All men are liars."

Dread, likewise, to think evil of him, for from the hour that this species of iniquity enters the heart, all love is destroyed.

The Scribes and Pharisees judged, and the Spirit of mercy abandoned them, so that they did not even know what was that Spirit.

The Scribes and Pharisees judged, and when they had discovered a guilty woman, they made known her fault, and demanded for her all the rigour of the law.

The Scribes and Pharisees judged, and when they were in the temple, they advanced to the sanctuary, and, holding themselves upright, they loaded with reproaches those who prayed and were kneeling near the portal of the temple.

They judged, and when a sinful woman of the city washed My feet and dried them with her hair, their hearts were seized with a strange astonishment and a secret indignation.

They judged, and when they met with men who did not follow the practices they had imposed on themselves, they repulsed them as prevaricators and sinners.

Truly, do I say unto thee, do thou beware

of resembling the Scribes and Pharisees, for hardness of heart is the chastisement of him who judges.

My son, do thou now proceed to the mountain of sacrifice, and speak, what dost thou there see, and what dost thou hear?

The Disciple.—O, my Master! I see men who respond to Thy looks with a sinister mien, their hands are armed with swords, and from their breasts escape piercing cries.

And these men were of that people who had contemplated Thy divine face, and the same who had said: "Hosanna! blessed is He who cometh in the name of the Lord!"

And I hear Thee, O, Master! and Thou sayest: "Father, they know not what they do."

I see men abetting each other mutually in their insensate rage, this one despoils Thee of Thy garments, this other extends Thy members, and that other again pierces them in uttering ferocious mockeries.

And these men were of that people who had heard all those words of love that proceeded from Thy lips, and who had said: "Hosanna to the Son of David, blessed is He who cometh in the name of the Lord!"

And I hear Thee, O, Master! and Thou dost say: "Father, they know not what they do."

I see men who present to Thee wine mingled with gall, this one opens Thy side with a lance, and another shakes his head, saying: "Thou, who wouldst destroy the temple of God, and rebuild it in three days, do Thou save Thyself;" and this other likewise shakes his head, saying: "If Thou be the Son of God, descend from the cross."

And these men were of that people that had seen the prodigies of Thy right hand, the cure of the blind and of the deaf, the resurrection of the dead, and who had said: "Blessed be that reign which comes, the reign of David our father, Hosanna in excelsis!"

And I hear Thee once more, O Master, and Thou dost say: "O Father, they know not what they do!"

The Master.—My son, thou hast seen distinctly, thou has heard aright, remember this vision, and comprehend My word.

It is the word of Him who thinketh not evil, and who would not judge.

II.

The Master.—My son, do not thou complain if men have not listened to thy voice; for thou hast not first walked in the straight paths.

It is not the word which should precede the example, but the example which should precede all words.

Thou spokest of love, and thy tongue was like

to a two-edged sword, and thy teeth were as arms and as sharp arrows.

Thou didst speak of love, and the venom of asps was on thy lips, and bitterness and gall flowed therefrom.

Thou didst speak of love, and thy words were as burning coals; at times they seemed endowed with the sweetness of honey, and they were but poisoned darts.

My son, men shall hear thy voice, but let not thy mouth be as an open sepulchre, exhibiting objects of horror, and exhaling odours of infection.

I have said unto thee, prepare thy heart, and judge not; and now I say unto thee, do thou prepare thy heart, and speak not evil of thy brother.

He who offends not by the tongue is perfect; and the voice of him who is perfect is at all times listened to.

Perfection is love in its true sense, and love is never fruitless, but produces with might, and the rays of heat it sends forth are blessed.

Do thou make a covenant with thine eyes, that they may not see the weakness of thy brothers, and make a covenant with thy lips, that they may not move to speak of them.

In vain thou wouldst seek to establish harmony amongst men if thou wilt not thus act; for the evil tongue stirs up tempests and carries desolation into all places.

It is as a fountain of bitter waters, which turns

away all creatures from the sources that spring up to eternal life.

Who is he whose tongue is evil? Is it not he who reveals the secret faults of his brother, and who would make them seem more grievous than they are in effect?

Is it not he who, seeing his brother go to and fro, now raise his eyes, anon cast them down, stand still, and then proceed on, is it not he who gives an evil interpretation to all these actions?

Who is he whose tongue is evil? Is it not he whose countenance becomes sad, and whose voice is silent when he hears the eulogy of the virtues and the works of his brother?

Is it not he who makes the malicious word pass under the guise of malignant praise? his features are more unctious than oil, but they are cutting as the sword.

Truly do I say unto thee, beware of resembling those who thus act, for evil words are not uttered in vain.

And do not these men constitute themselves the judges of the law, and is not their sin counted amongst the crimes that exclude from the kingdom of heaven?

He who spares not his brother in his words severs himself from him, for he provokes within his heart a spirit of hatred and vengeance.

This spirit he excites, inasmuch as he takes away a good which surpasses all others.

What are treasures, or what signifies love or life?

Thou hast seen some men expose their riches,

thou hast seen others sacrifice them, and others again spurn them, as though the contact of gold would sully their hands.

But that man who no longer clings to honour, hast thou seen him?

Thou hast beheld men renounce the joys of love, and go far from country, family, friends, with the view to obtain some noble end worthy of their hearts.

But the man who no longer esteems honour, him hast thou seen?

Thou hast seen men bestow that life they had received from on high, and bestow it easily, as though they deemed it little worth.

But he who no longer cherishes honour, hast thou seen him?

Truly, there are men who forfeit their honour, because they do evil works; but even those do not believe they have lost it.

And whensoever they hear a voice that condemns them, they revolt against themselves, and against that voice.

Therefore, do thou spare thy brother, provoke not within him the spirit of hatred and vengeance, for when thou wilt have created that spirit, how canst thou destroy it?

He who reveals the disgrace of his brother in his words severs himself from those who hear him, inasmuch as he excites within them the spirit of fear.

He has spread abroad sarcasm and raillery, he relishes the blood in which his lips are still dyed, but because his lips are dyed in blood, behold how he is charged with the universal abomination.

His poignant sallies have excited a smile; but, behold how revolt and indignation have succeeded the smile.

The satisfaction of an instant, the joy that his piercing darts may have given, shall have engendered a deadly horror.

Each one has said: "This man is formidable, let us fly his presence, for to-day he has made a victim, and to-morrow he shall make another.

"To-day it was this other; to-morrow it may be my turn."

Each one has said: "He has risen up against the divinities of the earth, against constituted authority, which claims by right man's submission and homage.

"He has avenged himself for his dependance by the licence of his censures, he has pursued the anointed of the Lord in searching out their failings, in exhibiting their weaknesses.

"How may we escape the malignity of his tongue, and the sharpness of his tooth?"

Each one has said: "He has profaned the sepulchres of the dead; like to a reptile, he has tightened his folds around their insensible bones, he has shed his venomous slaver over cold ashes.

"He has inveighed against virtue itself, he has treated it with greater severity and rigour than men use against vice, and ignominy, and crime.

"How may we escape the malignity of his tongue, and the sharpness of his teeth?"

All said amongst themselves: "The husband and the wife loved each other, brothers lived in peace, friends sustained each other; he passed his way, and love, and concord, and unity, are no more.

"He has passed amidst us, and shall we enjoy peace to-morrow?"

All said amongst themselves: "The child enjoyed his innocence, the virgin her modesty, the aged man the fruits of his labours; he has passed, and the child, the young maiden, and the aged man have ceased to enjoy.

"He has passed, and the innocent has been judged criminal, the modest maiden a guilty courtesan, and the old man has been reputed unjust.

"He has passed in the midst of us, and to-morrow shall we have joy, and honour, and peace?

"Shall the price of our daily toil, of our sufferings, and of our struggles, rest in our hands, when his tongue shall have crushed our bones?"

All have said: "No one may escape his venom; none can turn aside the point of his sword, for he has studied in the dark the perfidious art of imposing on men his wicked falsehoods.

"Some he persuades by the assured tones of his voice, to others he presents suspicions as certainties, and he boldly mingles the truth with the falsehood.

"To these he makes a gesture, to those he

replies with a smile, and he conveys more than he will express.

"And if he should pass amidst us, shall we have peace to-morrow?"

All have said amongst themselves: "One day he transforms virtues into those vices which they most resemble.

"According to his words, courage is but rashness, modesty is meanness, and reserve is but dissimulation.

"And then another day he disguises his sharp arrows under the language of friendship. With a semblance of sadness, he pities him whom he lacerates, and invests him with his hypocritical pity.

"Another day, again, he embellishes his victim with perfidious eulogies, but only in order to immolate him, and to pierce him with an arrow hidden amidst flowers.

"And if he should pass amidst us to-morrow, shall we not be betrayed with a kiss?"

Men have said amongst themselves: "He has ranged himself in the ranks of the perfect, and we have seen him assume humility of manner and modesty of mien.

"We have heard his voice, it was, as it were, broken with sobs, and from his breast escaped profound sighs, he hesitated to speak, and still he hesitated.

"And the voice became less broken, and the sighs more faint, and the condemnation of his fallen brother was spoken out.

"And then the groans recommenced, and the tears fell from his eyes, as though there could be compassion where there was no more love."

And all said amongst themselves: "If this man should pass in the midst of us to-morrow, shall we still believe in virtue?"

O, My son! reveal not the shame of thy brother, lest those who listen to thee should thereby become estranged from thee.

Do not create within them the spirit of fear; for, having once produced that spirit, how mayest thou destroy it?

Vainly thou wouldst seek their dwelling, they would flee at thy approach, they would leave their tabernacles deserted.

In vain thou wouldst speak to conduct them into the true path; they would reply: "We have heard thy voice, and we feared."

III.

The Disciple.—O, Master! who shall place a guard on my mouth, who shall set a secure seal on my lips, that my tongue may not prove my perdition, and that it may not render unavailing the words of truth and of justice that I would announce unto men?

They who pursue honours, and whom ambition agitates without ceasing, do not always abandon themselves to gross pleasures.

They who seek in their senses their joy and their happiness are not always solicitous to elevate themselves above others, or to subject them to their dominion.

They who attach their hearts to heaps of gold and of silver, are not always tormented by the pride of the spirit and by the rage of the flesh.

But, lo! I hear the prophet exclaim: "They are all gone aside, they are become unprofitable together; there is none that doth good, no, not one, their throat is an open sepulchre, with their tongues they acted deceitfully; the poison of asps is under their lips. Their mouth is full of cursing and bitterness."

O, Master! how shall I escape this abyss into which all descend? Who shall set a guard on my mouth, who shall place a secure seal on my lips?

The Master.—It is thine own heart which shall set a guard on thy mouth, and a gate of circumspection on thy lips.

Do thou destroy therein all sentiment of vengeance and hatred, and thou shalt render it powerful against thy words.

Thou has learned that it is said: "Thou shalt love thy neighbour, and hate thine enemy; but I say unto all men: Love your enemies, do good to those who hate you, pray for those who persecute you."

Thou must accustom thy heart to a holy insensibility in regard to injuries, so as not to be easily offended, that so it may not be troubled by any external thing.

If thy brother should displease thee, do not regard the action alone of which he has been guilty, but consider that it is not a stranger who has wounded thy heart.

Bear in mind that it is thy brother, and let this name recall to thee that his blood is the same as thine own, and that he is sustained by the same earth, and is warmed by the same sun.

Say not within thee: "I confided to him a secret, and he has betrayed me; I succoured him in his distress, and he has despised me; I gave myself to him, and he has abandoned me."

Say not these things, or thy spirit would be troubled, and thy heart be consumed by the flames of indignation and anger.

Do thou stifle the sentiment of hatred in its principle, and if thou wilt not, it will increase every hour, and become like to the great waters that are stirred up beneath the sway of the winds.

And if thou hast suffered this sentiment to enter thy heart, do thou not be discouraged, for My charity urges thee.

Seek not in thy weakness a force to oppose to the strength of My doctrine; for My Father who is in heaven commands not those things which are impossible to the children of men.

Abandoned to thyself, thou art inefficient and weak; but when thou art with Me, dost thou not feel thyself invested with My strength, as though it were with a buckler?

Do thou glory in thine infirmity, that My virtue

may dwell with thee; and fear not to fall under the weight of the burden, for I extinguish all hatred within souls of good will, more easily than thou canst a burning coal.

I have said unto thee: Love thine enemies, and pardon all injuries; and I shall now confirm thee by a promise.

Render not evil for evil, nor outrage for outrage; but repay evil and outrage by blessings, as knowing that it is to this thou art called, to the end that thou mayest receive the inheritance of the benediction of God.

Truly do I say unto thee, thou shalt receive this inheritance, for it is written, that it shall be meted unto thee in the same proportion as thou shalt have meted unto others.

When the tumult of the world around thee is stilled, and when thou wilt descend into the solitude of thy soul, dost thou not perceive that she has received the wounds of time, and that works of iniquity rise to her surface?

And, therefore, it is needful that thou shouldst repair these wounds, and disperse the dust of these works by sacrifice; and sacrifice means to say humiliation, and the greatest of all humiliations, is it not in a word of pardon?

O, My son! do thou deposit this humiliation in My hands, even as I deposited in the hands of My Heavenly Father, for the salvation of all, the humiliation of My last sigh.

Consequently, when thou comest to present thy offering at the altar, and when thou rememberest that thy brother is offended with thee, do thou leave thine offering before the altar, and go first and reconcile thyself with thy brother.

Hasten to make peace with thine enemy, whilst thou art still with him in the path of life, lest he should deliver thee up to the Sovereign Judge, and lest the Judge should deliver thee over to the evil one, who is the minister of His justice.

My son, do thou listen on, and comprehend this parable:

"The kingdom of heaven is likened to a king who would take an account of his servants.

"And when he had begun to take the account, one was brought to him that owed him ten thousand talents.

"And as he had not wherewith to pay it, his lord commanded that he should be sold, and his wife and children, and all that he had, and payment to be made.

"But the servant, falling down, besought him, saying: Have patience with me, and I will pay thee all.

"And the lord of that servant, being moved with pity, let him go, and forgave him the debt.

"But when the servant was gone out, he found one of his fellow-servants that owed him a hundred pence; and, laying hold of him, he throttled him, saying: Pay me what thou owest.

"And his fellow-servant, falling down, besought him, saying: Have patience with me, and I will pay thee all.

"And he would not; but went and cast him into prison till he paid the debt.

"Now his fellow-servants, seeing what was done, were very much grieved, and they came and told their lord all that was done.

"Then his lord called him, and said to him: Thou wicked servant, I forgave thee all the debt, because thou besoughtest me; shouldst not thou then have had compassion also on thy fellow-servant, even as I had compassion on thee?

"And his lord, being angry, delivered him to the torturers, until he paid all the debt."

So also shall My Heavenly Father do to you, if you forgive not everyone his brother from your hearts.

O thou, who wouldst seek to establish harmony on earth, abstain from the words of condemnation, for it is not within the power of him who cherishes hatred to perform the works of love.

Having destroyed those works within his own heart, how may he bestow that which he no longer possesses?

Banish hatred, and thy tongue shall cease to carry desolation into all places, it shall cease to stir up tempests, or to be like to a fountain of bitter waters.

Do thou banish hatred from thee, for it shall reveal itself in spite of thee, there are no chains it does not rend, no walls it does not overthrow; woe to him who surprises it in its revelations, for he shall listen to thee no more.

O, My son! the hour will come when I will

teach thee to pardon other men, in the name of My Father, the sins committed against My Father.

But previously to that hour thou must have already created within thee entrails of mercy, in order to pardon thy brothers their trangressions against thee.

Shall thy brother comprehend that spirit of mercy that abides within the heart of thy Heavenly Father, if he sees not in thy heart, as it were, the image of that spirit?

Do thou present to him this vision, and he shall be consoled, and in his joy he shall exclaim:

"Because mercy is to be found in Thy saints, I have, O Lord, believed in Thy pardon."

IV.

The Disciple.—O Master! I have preserved my heart from hatred, but my tongue has not been exempt from sin; I have pardoned all those who had risen up against me, but my word retained the sharpness of the sword.

O, Master! who shall place a seal on my mouth, and a gate of circumspection on my lips?

The Master.—My son, I have descended into thy heart, I have viewed all its fibres, and these fibres were strained.

And that which thus strained them was a secret

anguish, and I alone beheld that anguish, I whose glance pierces into the abysses.

A weight of sadness was within thee, but wherefore wast thou sad?

Because thine eyes had contemplated the prosperity, and the glory, and the virtue of thy brother.

And why were the features of thy face altered, as those of a man who has passed through great anguish?

Because thine ears had been struck by the clamour of the multitude that acclaimed a glory that was not thine own.

And then, because sadness had entered thy heart, flaming darts have issued from thy mouth.

Wouldst thou set a gate of prudence on thy lips? then arise, and shake off thy sadness, impose silence on thy lamentations.

Even as I have said unto thee, chase away the spirit of hatred and vengeance, so do I say unto thee now, chase away all spirit of envy.

He who cherishes that spirit, is he not like to the angels of darkness? Behold those angels, how they transport themselves hither and thither, and from one place to another, in search of some prey.

And is it not because they are jealous of the children of men?

They assumed the garb of the serpent, and it was because they would impede their beatitude.

They clothed themselves with the splendour of the angels of light, and it was because they would wrest from their hands the inheritance that was promised them.

And he who cherishes that spirit, does he not revolt against the doctrine of My works, and against these same works?

I charged Myself with the infirmities and with the wants of the children of men, and I imparted to them My gifts and My virtues.

And he who nourishes the spirit of envy, would he not fain give to his brother his own weakness and misery, and claim for himself all glory and honour?

I came in order to establish a vast society of souls, bound together by the might and the power of love.

And he who nourishes the spirit of envy, does he not come to break the bonds of that union of souls?

Does he not sever himself from all his brothers whom he sees more favoured than himself?

Listen, thou, and comprehend: behold the vision of the prophet.

The prophet beheld issuing forth from the waters of the sea four wild animals.

And the first of these was a lioness, with the wings of an eagle; and the second was a bear, with three rows of teeth in his jaws.

And the third animal was a winged leopard; and the fourth, to this he could not give a name.

He was unlike the three other beasts, he gnawed with his teeth all that he could crunch, and he trampled underfoot that which he could not gnaw.

On his head were eleven horns, the last of these was smaller than the others, and he had the eyes of a man.

And if thou sayest that envy is represented by the first of these animals, thou art not mistaken.

For does she not will to domineer over all things, and reign as does the lion amongst the terrestrial beasts, and as the eagle amidst the birds of the air?

And if thou dost say that envy is represented by the second of these animals, thou wilt have said aright.

Even as the bear is troubled, and becomes dazzled when he meets with some shining object, even so is not the envious man internally troubled when he beholds in his brother glory and virtue?

And shouldst thou say that envy is portrayed in the third of these animals, again thou wilt have said aright.

Do not the specks of the leopard represent the dissimulation and suppleness with which the envious man forges, as it were, spears and poisoned darts.

And if thou dost say that envy is pictured by the fourth of these animals, thou shalt have still more rightly spoken, and the truth shall be on thy lips.

Is not envy dissimilar from all other passions?

The ambitious and the luxurious pursue glory

or pleasure; but the envious man tortures himself, forasmuch as he abandons glory for baseness, and prefers bitterness to joy.

As that animal that gnaws all he encounters, behold how the envious man gnaws with malignant tooth all the garments of his brother.

The bear and the leopard have stood still before him who flung them their prey.

The rage of the lion has been appeased before him who has fascinated him by the power and the fixedness of his glance.

But the envious man descends beneath the rank of the fiercest of animals.

No prey suffices for him, no glance appeases him.

He raises his head against goodness and tenderness, because all virtue excites within him a new thirst which consumes him.

He has lost his peace, therefore, why should his trouble not betray him?

He has lost all love, and how should his word not bring death?

Truly do I say unto thee: do thou destroy that spirit which awakes within thee insensate desires, whose eternal lamentations corrupt thine heart.

When thy brother is in glory and honour, why shouldst thou suffer anguish to descend into thy soul?

Are not the glory and the honour of thy brother as though they were thine own?

He has elevated himself by the conceptions of

his genius, he has triumphed by his valour, he has shone by the wisdom of his works.

And hast thou not thy part in this elevation of his, and in these his triumphs?

He has felt anguish seize him in the very depths of his soul, and he has felt sorrow succeed to his joys.

He has seen his elevation disappear as the smoke that arises from the fiery furnace, he has seen his triumphs vanish away.

But wherefore should thine heart throb with exultation?

Are not the humiliations and the sorrows of thy brother as though they were thine own?

You are the members of the same body, and if one of those should suffer, dost thou not know that it is written that all the other members shall likewise suffer?

And if one of those members be in joy, knowest thou not that it is also written that all the others should in like manner rejoice?

When thy brother ascends from virtue to virtue because he follows the light, and because he hears all the words that come from on high, wherefore, then, shouldst thou be afflicted?

Does not his virtue protect thy weakness and thy misery? and does not his strength become as it were thine own?

Forasmuch as I have said: "And the glory which Thou hast given Me, I have given to them, that they may be one, as We also are One;"

Do thou rejoice in those gifts I have bestowed

on thy brother, and thou shalt then partake of these same gifts; do thou rejoice in the good he effects, and that good shall be, as it were, thine own work.

It shall descend on thy poverty as fruitful dew-drops, because the prayers and the lamentations of the just traverse all space.

They shall dilate on all sides, they shall repose on all creatures, because they have ascended to Me, and have been blessed by My hand.

The Disciple.—O Master, I have heard the poor man complain and lament in seeing the abundance of the rich, and I have heard the rich man likewise complain, because his treasures increased not as those of his brothers.

I have seen the learned of this world rise up against each other, jealous of those laurels their own hands had not culled.

I have seen those who were placed in the ranks of the perfect, and these men seemed to despise the prosperity and the wealth of this earth. But behold how they were consumed by the desire of the fame and the praise of their virtue.

They lamented when their counsels were not regarded as oracles, and when others performed works which were extolled by the world.

These things I have witnessed, and, as desiring the perfection of the perfect, I became troubled, and exclaimed: O Master, how shall I act?

The Master. — The poor, the rich, and the learned have grown sad; thou hast heard them as they murmured, for pride had corroded their hearts.

The poor would be the equal of the rich, and the rich coveted the opulence of him who was still richer than he, and the learned man despised his own glory, as perceiving that there were other glories still greater than his.

They who had ranged themselves in the ranks of the perfect were troubled, and thou hast heard their murmurs, for pride had likewise corroded their hearts.

Whereas they had not made unto themselves idols of gold, or of silver, or of wood, or of flesh, they believed they adored *Him who is* in spirit and in truth, and, nevertheless, they worshipped themselves.

O My son! be thou humble, and I shall give thee My joy, and thou shalt not be consumed by the insensate desires that turn men aside from the ways of love.

Then thy tongue shall cease to be as a two-edged sword; nor shall thy teeth be as sharp and cutting arrows.

Then thou shalt speak, and sin shall be no longer in thy words; for in witnessing the glory of thy brother thy heart shall exclaim:

"I have preserved my peace, and I have dilated my joy."

FOURTH COLLOQUY.

THE MASTER INSTRUCTS HIS DISCIPLE HOW TO UNITE WITH HIS BROTHERS BY EXTERIOR ACTS. — HE TEACHES HIM HOW HE SHOULD LISTEN TO THOSE WHO NEED CONSOLATION, AND HOW HE SHOULD SPEAK TO THEM.—THE MASTER LIKEWISE TEACHES THE DISCIPLE HOW TO SOLACE THE DISINHERITED OF THE GOODS OF THIS EARTH, SO AS TO PREPARE THE HEARTS OF ALL WHO SUFFER TO LISTEN TO THE WORDS OF LIFE.

FOURTH COLLOQUY.

I.

The Disciple.—I have left judgment to Him who sounds the hearts and the loins, and whose glance penetrates all things, past, present, and to come.

I have set a gate of circumspection upon my lips in destroying within me the spirit of hatred, of vengeance, and of envy.

Behold how I have levelled the wall of separation which I had raised, behold how my brothers shall never again say when seeing me:

"If he should pass in the midst of us to-morrow, shall we enjoy peace?"

And now, O Master, will men not hearken to my voice?

The Master.—My son, they shall hearken to thy voice if they know that thou lovest them, and they will believe in thy love if thou wilt endeavour to appease all sorrow within them.

Sin has entered the world, and with sin death and suffering; and suffering has penetrated all flesh.

It has passed into the substance of all creatures, it has invaded all spirits and all bodies, and all creatures have groaned.

The child is acquainted with tears, the eye of the aged is wet; all weep, because tribulation sweeps again and again over every heart, and wrings every breast.

And behold how, in desiring to be heard by men, and to cast into them the seeds of light and of life, behold how I combated all anguish, all sadness.

I brought joy to little children, because I suffered them to draw near Me, I brought joy to the blind in giving them sight, and to the paralytics in saying to them: "Take up your bed and return to your house."

And the little children, and the blind, and the paralytics heard My voice.

My son, it has been said of the Son of Man that He shall not make exception of persons; now, I say unto thee, he in whom dwells the spirit of love, loves all his brothers without distinction.

He loves the rich, and he loves the poor, he loves the great and the little, he loves the learned and the unlearned.

Are not all the children of men equal before God? For does not His love extend from the greatest to the least, from the richest to the poorest?

Is there one alone for whom He has done less than He has for others, and over whom He watches with less of solicitude than over other men?

Has He displayed less of His power in creating the poor than He has in creating the rich?

Behold how thy heavenly Father has been just in the creation; He formed the first man out of the slime of the earth, He breathed into his face the breath of life; and the first man became living and animated.

And, from that day, have not all men received in the same proportion? Are not their bodies formed of the same slime, and is not the same breath of life diffused over their faces?

And the soul of the last of the children of men, is it not like unto that of the first man, that is to say, loving, intelligent, and immortal?

And are not the least equally capable as the greatest of knowing the Master of all things, of loving Him, of possessing Him, and of consummating their felicity in Him?

Behold, once more, how thy celestial Father was just in the redemption; did He not give His Son for all men? and I, that Eternal Son of the Father, I whom He engendered before all ages, did I not take the form of the servant, to suffer and to die for all those who groan under servitude?

Did I not come to bring salvation as well to the Gentiles as to the sons of Israel, to the Scythians and the barbarians, to free men and slaves?

Wherefore, then, shouldst thou make exception of persons, wherefore should thy heart open to some alone and not to all others?

Knowest thou not, then, that thou shouldst resemble thy heavenly Father? knowest thou not that thou shouldst walk in the footprints of thy Master?

And thy Master, is He not He who said: My blood is the blood of the new Covenant, which shall be shed for the salvation of all?

And thy Master, was it not He who said: I am come to instruct the poor, I shall choose all that is weakest and most miserable in the eyes of men, that I may confound the strong.

My love is alike for the great and for the little; and if I have displayed more of tenderness for these latter than for the first, it is because it is expedient to act so, that the world may understand that they who would be My disciples should divest themselves of the thoughts and the judgments of men, and bestow the same measure of love on all, whether little or great.

For do not all need to be treated with tenderness?

And is not the heart of the little and of the poor, is it not formed like unto that of the rich and the great? And if these latter revolt when one does not greet them with love, should not the poor, in like manner, revolt?

Have not the little their afflictions, their miseries and infirmities, and dost thou believe that because feeling themselves trampled on and despised, they should have grown hardened to all feeling?

If, at times, they err, and fall into grievous

crimes, it is not that they have lost all heart, but because their hearts have been crushed by the hardness of men.

They have been seen to suffer, and no one came to solace their sufferings, they have been seen to weep, and no one came to weep with them, they have groaned, and their groanings found no echo.

And behold how it is that their hearts, which had not been solaced by love, have been embittered within them, and they have said within themselves: "Let us shake off the chains which still bind us to duty, let us break our fetters, let us be revenged on those who have not loved us."

Truly do I say unto thee, they who make exception of persons love not, and do much evil.

Thou hearest with benevolence the recital made by the great of their tribulations and griefs.

Thou leavest thy affairs to give ear to their long discourses, and, even when they weary thee, thy face betrays no sign of sadness or weariness.

Thy lips give utterance to no sighs that repulse, thou dost violence to thine heart, so as to guard it in patience.

Why dost thou not so act with regard to the least of thy brethren?

The child of labour and the poor man, do they not still more need that thou shouldst open thy door to them?

And when one such comes to thee, if thou wouldst say to him: My friend, seat thyself beside me, and speak of thy sufferings, what joy should not enter his heart?

And, when perceiving that thou listenedst to the recital of his griefs, how immense should be his gratitude?

And having thus listened to him, what power wouldst thou not acquire over his soul, how welcome should be thy word!

My son, I have instructed thee in My ways; let thy love cease to be partial; do thou expand thy heart, for if thou wilt not do so it shall have no real love.

Now thou knowest that he who possesses not this love is sterile. He speaks, and his word is vain, he acts, and his actions alone bring death, when in effect they should impart life.

Till now thou didst believe thou couldst love in God, but thou hast loved irrespectively of Him, and behold the reason why thou hast been wanting to thy mission.

Thou shalt never truly love souls till that day when thou shalt render them service, and thou shalt never do so save in loving them as I have loved them.

For thee let there be no more exception of persons, for thee let there be no more of great or little, or rich or poor.

For what is love if it be not universal?

II.

The Master.—My son, if thou didst follow Me, behold that which thou didst see.

Thou sawest Me one day take the way to Jericho, and as I drew nigh to the city, a blind man who was seated by the way-side, hearing the rush of a multitude of people, demanded what this meant.

And being told that Jesus of Nazareth was passing by, he cried out: "Jesus, Son of David, have mercy on me!"

And they who went before rebuked him, that he would hold his peace, but he cried out much more: "Son of David, have mercy on me."

Thereupon I stood still, and made him be led to Me. And when he was come near Me, I asked him, saying: "What wilt thou that I do to thee?"

But he said: "Lord, that I may see." And I said to him: "Receive thy sight, thy faith hath made thee whole;" and immediately he saw, and followed Me, glorifying God.

If thou didst follow Me, behold again that which thou didst witness.

Thou didst see Me descend from the mountain, followed by a multitude of people, and at the same time a leper came and adored Me.

And, in adoring Me, he addressed Me this prayer: "Lord, if Thou wilt Thou canst make me clean."

I had compassion on this man, I stretched forth My hand, and, touching him, I said: "I will that thou be made clean."

And directly I had spoken, the leprosy of that man was cleansed.

Another day, a centurion had a sick servant who was in danger of death, and that servant was very dear to him.

Having heard of My repute, he came to Me and prayed Me to come and cure his servant.

I said to him: "I will come and heal him." And the centurion, making answer, said: "Lord, I am not worthy that Thou shouldst enter my roof, but only say the word, and my servant shall be healed."

Another day, again, there was presented to Me a man deaf and mute, who was possessed by an evil spirit.

And I drew near to that man, whom the evil one had rendered mute, and when I had chased away the demon, he who had been deaf and dumb spoke out.

The multitude were struck with admiration, and cried out: "His like has never been seen in Israel."

If thou didst follow Me, behold once more that which thou didst witness.

Thou sawest Me repair to a city called Naim, followed by My disciples, and a vast number of people.

And when I came nigh to the city, behold a dead man was carried out, the only son of his mother, and she was a widow, and many people of the city were with her.

And when I saw her, I had compassion on her. And I said to her: "Weep not." And I came near and touched the bier. And they that carried it stood still.

And I said: "Young man, I say to thee, arise," and he that was dead sat up and began to speak. And I delivered him to his mother.

And thus did I console the children of men, and thus I might say to the disciples of John: "Go and tell your master what you have heard and seen.

"That the blind see, that the lame walk, that the lepers are cleansed, that the deaf hear, that the dead rise again, and that the gospel is announced to the poor."

And because I consoled the children of men, in assuaging all their sufferings and their pains, behold how they came to Me publishing the greatness of God, and hearing My word.

The Disciple.—O Master, prodigies are in Thy hands, and Thou hast consoled each creature in his sorrow, but he who mourns within himself, he who weeps, what help may there be *in* him?

Do not his groans, do not his tears bespeak his weakness, his inefficiency, and if he knows not how to cure his own pains, how may he hope to cure other men?

The Master.—Has not the Son of Man groaned? Has He not wept?

Didst thou not see Him in His birth, didst

thou not see Him in His life and in His death, and didst thou not behold in Him the Man of Sorrows?

And if He worked prodigies with a view to the consolation of souls, wherefore shouldst thou not do so in like manner?

The prodigies which I have placed within thy reach, they lie not in the force of thine arm, they are within the centre of thy heart.

And be not troubled if the touch of thy fingers will not console the blind, in restoring him his sight, or if thou canst not console those who love, in rendering to them those who slept the sleep of death.

Open thine heart, and the blind, although still uncured, shall yet be consoled.

Open thine heart, and although the mother shall rest for evermore bereft of her child, although the brother shall never more behold the sister, nor the friend the cherished friend of his heart, yet, nevertheless, they shall be consoled.

O My son! behold how thou shalt open thy heart to him who suffers: thou shalt listen to him.

To listen to lamentations and to the recital of deep woe, it is to love; and to love is to bestow joy. Listen, listen long and frequently to that soul that speaks of her woe, and say not to her that thy hours are counted.

He who suffers is cured by that confidence he reposes in another man, but his confidence is like to the leaf of the tree, which slowly unfolds itself.

Do thou beware of arresting its growth by any agitation or fatigue thou mayest betray.

As the eye of the sick man seeks to read, in the countenance of him who approaches him, his sensations in beholding his pallid and altered features, even so does the mourner penetrate with anxiety each movement of his listener.

And if he should see that he is wearied of hearing him, he shall falter in speaking, and he shall quickly cease.

Learn from Me to bend thine ear to his plaints, in remembering My example.

When I drew nigh to the town of Jericho, whither I was repairing to preach the kingdom of God and His justice,

And whilst I was on the way I instructed the crowd that followed Me,

I was urged by a great desire to accomplish a mission, and the days and the nights were but too short.

But lo! thou didst hear the blind man exclaim: " Son of David, have mercy on me!"

Thou didst behold Me, and at that hour I listened.

And again, I encountered a ruler of the synagogue, who besought Me to enter his house, saying: "Lord, my only daughter is even now dead."

And did I not, in so doing, occupy Myself with the concerns of My Father?

And thou didst hear the afflicted man exclaim:

"Lord, come and lay Thy hand upon her, and she shall live."

Thou didst behold Me, and at that hour I listened.

Another day, as I traversed Samaria and Galilee, I entered a village, and ten lepers passed the way.

And did I not then occupy Myself with the concerns of My Father?

And thou didst hear these lepers raise their voices, exclaiming: "Jesus, our Master, take pity on us!"

Thou didst behold Me, and at that hour I listened.

And when the plaint of thy brother reaches thee, do thou likewise bend thine ear, and say not that duty presses thee, for duty consists in loving.

When thou dost repair from one place to another, if thou shouldst encounter some unfortunate, and if that unfortunate should desire to speak with thee, do thou stop on thy way, and listen to him.

If thou shouldst be in company with thy friend, and thou shouldst meet with some afflicted man, and if that unhappy man should desire to speak with thee, do thou leave thy friend and listen to him who suffers.

Or, art thou absorbed in thy occupation, and eager to complete it? Truly, do I say unto thee, if a man should present himself to thee, wishing to speak to thee of his tribulations, do thou leave thy occupations, and listen to him who is afflicted.

Woe to him who knows not how to stop on his way, to abandon his friend's society, or to leave his occupation, for that man in closing his ear shall have likewise closed his heart.

He shall have rendered sterile the power which I have placed within him, and his brother shall go his way because he will not have dried his tears.

O My son! behold once more how thou shouldst open thy heart to him who suffers. When thou shalt have heard him, thou shalt speak.

It is written, that death is within the power of the tongue; but it is likewise written, that life is placed within its power.

Thou hast seen that the malicious word separates brother from brother, but do thou now learn that words of tenderness are productive of unity and joy.

There are within the spirit of him who weeps secret griefs which will not reveal themselves unasked, and which durst not ascend from the depths of the soul, nor show themselves in that light which might dissipate them.

These secret woes, do thou search them out by a friendly word, and they shall cease to dread the power of thy glance.

Thy love has been already revealed to the unfortunate, forasmuch as thou hast listened to his plaints, but it shall reveal itself still more, if thou wilt respond to his anguish.

He has bent towards thee, and thou hast not repulsed him, do thou bend down towards him, and then he shall seize thine hand, that thou mayest touch, in the depths of his heart, his most hidden wound.

And now, is it not the word of friendship that responds to anguish, that inclines one soul towards another soul?

Is it not that same which diffuses over the tenderness that dwells within the solitude of the heart, as it were, a luminous ray, that it may become visible to eyes of flesh?

Therefore do thou question him who suffers, and endeavour to see into his soul, as one sees into a pure and transparent water.

It is then thou wilt remove, one by one, those sharp stones that wound him along his way, and which are within him as a heavy burden oppressing him and impeding his steps.

He shall answer thee, forasmuch as he needs to answer thee; he shall answer thee, for he shall have already felt still closer to him the throbbings of thy heart, and discovered that he is no longer alone.

And when thou shalt have seen his latest sorrow, in his last reply, do thou not yet cease to speak.

The avowal of suffering is the commencement of consolation; nevertheless, it is not consolation in its plenitude.

Speak to him, and make him comprehend that all sadness endures but for a time, and that joy comes after sorrow.

Thou shalt dilate his soul, because thou shalt have inspired it with hope; and all who hope already find within them the force to sustain the weight of the meridian heat.

And then, as though human things flitted before his eyes as ships driven before the storm—then shall he see that all creatures are hastening onwards to a land of stability, and that passing suffering may not arrest their career.

Do thou speak, and make him comprehend that there is not one man on earth, even to the infant of a day, who is pure from blemish, and that expiation lies in suffering, forasmuch as all sadness purifies.

Thou shalt infuse light into his mind, and in the rays of that light he shall comprehend the counsels of heaven.

And then shall he present his tears to My Father, as an expiatory sacrifice, and they shall be less bitter; and he shall sustain the weight of his woes as a yoke that is both easy and sweet.

Do thou speak, and make him comprehend that suffering is the principle and the bulwark of virtue.

Thou shalt infuse into his mind a second light, and in the rays of that light he shall see that terrestrial joy is in the hands of men as a fiery steed in the hands of a child, and as is a rudder in those of an unskilful pilot.

Then he shall not raise his voice against tribulation, because he shall understand why present and passing bliss has not come to visit his heart.

Then shall he discover a certain sweetness in that which seemed to him heretofore as bitter, because he shall have found the force to say within himself: Lord, it is salutary for me that Thou shouldst have humbled me.

Do thou speak, and make him comprehend that I formed My disciples not in repose and in peace, but in contradiction and in sorrow.

Thou shalt infuse a third light into his spirit, and in the beams of that light he shall see that suffering is the heritage of all who love and who follow Me.

Then shall it be given him to comprehend these words of Mine: Blessed are they who weep, blessed are they who suffer persecution for justice sake.

Truly, truly, he shall comprehend them, and in presence of this other word which I have spoken: "The world shall be in joy, and thou shalt be in sadness," his heart shall not be troubled.

He shall have seen through thy means joy in affliction, he shall have seen repose amidst toil, and affliction and toil shall be for him, as it were, a vision which fortifies.

III.

The Disciple.—O, Master, when I shall have listened to the lamentations of those who suffer, and when I shall have responded to these lamentations, as Thou hast said, will men then hear my voice?

The Master.—It is written, a glass of water given in My name shall not be left without its reward.

Do thou comprehend this word, do thou reduce it to practice, and men shall hear thy voice.

Thou didst not close thine ears to their plaints, thou wast not silent when they wept, and behold how they are already united with thee!

Do thou render perfect that union by the works of thy hands. Give to eat to him who is hungry, and give to drink to him who is thirsty.

He who loves bestows himself; but if thus it be, whence comes it that he cannot bestow exterior things which are within his power?

Is not the sacrifice he makes of these external things the commencement of that act by which he wills to bestow his spirit and his heart with his whole self?

I have shed down on the sons of men afflictions and sadness which thy word can solace, but which thy word alone cannot dissipate.

Can the hungry be satiated by words, or can the naked be clothed by the sounds of thy voice?

Thou hast learned to listen and to speak, do thou likewise learn to act.

It is written, that a certain man went down from Jerusalem to Jericho, and fell among robbers, who had stripped him, and having wounded him, went away, leaving him half dead.

And it chanced that a certain priest went down the same way, and, seeing him, passed by.

In like manner also, a Levite, when he was near the place, and saw him, passed by.

But a certain Samaritan being on his journey, came near him, and seeing him, was moved with compassion.

And, going up to him, bound up his wounds, pouring in oil and wine, and setting him upon his own beast, brought him to an inn, and took care of him.

And the next day he took out two pieces and gave to the host, and said:

"Take care of him, and whatsoever thou shalt spend over and above, I, at my return, will repay thee."

My son, thou art that Samaritan passing the way: do thou act in like manner.

Indigence and nudity are to be found on thy path; consequently, receive into thy house him who is without shelter, clothe him who is naked, and give bread to the hungry.

The substance of the poor is within the hands of the rich, and thy heavenly Father has confided to thee the indigent as a portion of His people that is dear unto Him.

They have said: "What shall we do? what shall become of us? Behold, we are about to perish."

And they have said: "Where shall we find aliments to sustain existence? Where shall we find the raiment needful for hiding our nakedness?"

And hear how thy Father, who is in heaven, replied to that cry of distress: "I shall fill all those who are hungry, I shall open My granaries, and I shall call to Me all those who are indigent."

And if He answers thus, is it not in order to place this reply on thy lips, is it not to guide thy hand to the door of thy granaries?

The poor are fallen into depression and sorrow, and they have said a second time: "What shall we do? what will become of us?"

And hear thou My reply to the rich: Do you feed them, and it is I whom you shall feed, do you clothe them, and it is I whom you shall clothe.

It is I who dwell in those dark retreats that you despise, and in those infected dwellings where you would not lodge the very beasts that serve you.

It is I who am weak, and pallid, and naked, and these wounds that you will not touch, and from which you turn away your eyes, these wounds are Mine.

Say not: "The times are hard, and our substance is scarcely sufficient for us, and how might we feed the hungry and cover the naked?"

And when the times are hard for him who sows and who reaps, are they not still more so for him who neither sows nor reaps?

The times are hard, and your garments have lost none of their splendour, and you pamper your bodies with luxuries, and your pleasures have found no limits.

And, if so it be, do you not delude yourselves in saying: "How may we sustain him who is hungry, or clothe him who is naked?"

Say not: "No one is poor save through his own fault;" for there is an indigence which proceeds neither from idleness or from excess.

Truly, I say unto you, your heavenly Father permits that there should be indigence, in order to exercise the mercy of the rich.

Woe unto you, if you do not comprehend that you have been placed, in regard to the poor, like as it were to a maternal bosom, to sustain them with your substance.

Neither say you: "Blasphemy is on their lips, they reject the truth as though it might hurt them, they drink iniquity as water, and they exclaim: 'We have sinned, and what evil has accrued to us therefrom?'

"How, O Lord, may we succour the impious, how may we love those who despise Thy law and blaspheme Thy name?"

If they be evil, do you convert them in being yourselves still more evil than they?

Thou who hast the true doctrine and the true purity, do thou act so as that they may not say: What avail truth and justice, if love dwell not in the midst of them?

The indigent comprehends truth but through love, and he comprehends love, alone when receiving.

Do thou sate his hunger and cover his nakedness, and thou wilt have cast into his mind a ray of light, and into his heart a germ of virtue.

There are men who say: "We have drawn nigh to the poor man who blasphemes, and our hand has been extended to aid him.

"He has received silver and gold, and wine and bread, yet he has not amended."

And these become sad, and sadness stops their ears, and turns aside their hearts from the ways of love.

Truly, truly, do I say unto thee, imitate them not; but do thou give a first time, give a second time, give without ceasing.

As thy heavenly Father hears him who is not wearied of crying out, even so the poor man will hear him who is not tired of bestowing.

O, My son, lose not courage, and comprehend this word of consolation: Charity covers a multitude of sins.

When alone with thyself thou dost pass in review all thine iniquities, behold how a holy and salutary fear overwhelms thee; do thou bestow some portion of thy substance, and these fears shall be dispelled.

For do not alms ascend like prayer to the throne of thy heavenly Father, and do they not descend again with the words of pardon?

Thou hast distributed perishable riches, and they have been transformed into a treasure which shall never be wrested from thee.

O, My son, lose not courage, and comprehend this other word of consolation: Better is it to give than to receive.

Thou hast received life, and life is a benefit; and thy heart has been wearied by the succession of the days and the nights.

Thou hast received glory, and honour, and praise, and it would seem to thee that in receiving these things thou shouldst have found a great joy.

And thine heart has become wearied of glory, of honour, and of praise.

The blossoms that decked the fields have been transformed into fruits, and these fruits have ripened to refresh thy lips.

The branches of the vine have been spread out, they have been filled with a strengthening liquor; and when the chills of the winter arrived, that liquor has warmed thy members.

And thou hast not found in the abundance of these boons the force to sustain the weight of the day.

But, behold this man on the point of death, thy brow has bent over him, thy hand has succoured him, and behold how thy dejected heart has been raised by consolation.

Truly do I say unto thee, amongst all the boons which I bestow in this life on the children of men, not one renders them content, forasmuch as I have placed in the estrangement from these goods the only true joy.

And this true joy is the treasure of him who leaves his solitude to unite with his brothers; and he who bestows has already commenced that union.

He quits his solitude as a barren desert, and walks already over fertile fields, watered by fountains of pure water, and reflecting the warm beams of the sun.

IV.

The Master.—My son, behold My works, and thou shalt dilate thine heart.

The earth was opened to bring Me forth. I came as the angel of a new covenant, in order to complete the union of men with My Father, and to unite them amongst themselves.

I came down from the eternal hills, where I reposed in My splendour and in My glory, that I might preach the kingdom of God and His justice.

And behold how thou didst see Me console all manner of sorrow, restore sight to the blind, hearing to the deaf, and raise the dead to life.

And behold, again, how thou didst see Me feed

the hungry, lest they might faint away in those places where they followed Me to listen to My words.

One day, being accompanied by a multitude of people, I repaired to the mountain, where I seated Myself down with My disciples, and I began to instruct this multitude concerning various matters.

I spoke to them of the kingdom of God, and I restored health to them who stood in need of being cured.

The day being far advanced, My disciples spoke to Me these words: "This place is not inhabited, and the hour is already past, dismiss them that they may procure victuals in the farms and in the villages."

And they said to Me: "Let us go and buy bread for two hundred pieces of money, and we shall give them to eat."

Thereupon, raising My eyes, and considering this vast concourse of people who came to Me, I said to Philip: "Whence may we buy bread that these may eat?"

And Philip answered; "Two hundred pennyworth is not sufficient for them, that every one may take a little.

One of My disciples, Andrew, the brother of Simon Peter, said to Me: "There is a boy here that hath five barley loaves and two fishes, but what are they among so many?"

And I then said: "Make the men sit down." Now there was much grass in the place. The men therefore sat down, in number about five thousand.

And I took the loaves, and when I had given thanks, I distributed to them that were sat down.

In like manner also the fishes, as much as they would; and when they were filled, I said to My disciples: "Gather up the fragments that remain, that nothing be lost."

They gathered up, therefore, and filled twelve baskets with the fragments of the five barley loaves which remained over and above to them that had eaten.

And these men, when they had seen what a miracle I had done, said: "This is of a truth the Prophet that is to come into the world."

O My son! preserve within thy heart the remembrance of this prodigy of My right hand, and learn to open thy hands to the wants of thy brother.

Fix not thine eyes on his guilty acts, but regard his indigence alone, so as to gain him by that substance with which thou wilt satiate his hunger.

If thou hast but one loaf, do thou divide that loaf, lest he should curse the day on which he saw the light, and lest his ears should close to every word of life.

Then he shall come to thee like to the newborn babe, who, knowing nothing beyond the bosom that has nourished him, sweetly smiling, extends his arms to his mother.

And then, understanding that truth is in the heart of him who loves, he shall listen to thy voice, and exclaim :

" Blessed be he who cometh in the name of the Lord !"

FIFTH COLLOQUY.

THE DISCIPLE DEMANDS TO BEAR TO SOULS THE WORD OF LIFE.—THE MASTER REPLIES TO HIM THAT THE HOUR IS COME WHEN HE MAY SPEAK.—HE INSTRUCTS HIM HOW TO GUARD HIS HEART IN PATIENCE.—HE COUNSELS HIM NOT TO BREAK THE BRUISED REED OR TO EXTINGUISH THE SMOKING TORCH.—THE MASTER TEACHES ALL THESE THINGS BY HIS EXAMPLE.

FIFTH COLLOQUY.

I.

The Master.—My son, I have taught thee not to separate men by judgments, or by the malignant word.

I have taught thee how thou shouldst unite thyself to them by words of consolation, and detachment from external goods.

Behold the hour when thou art to announce all truth and all virtue.

I have placed on thy lips the words of eternal life, therefore do thou speak to thy brothers now, and cease not to speak to them.

Clothe thyself with patience as with a buckler, for thou shalt have many combats to sustain.

Thou shalt undergo a multitude of labours and fatigues, and each day thou shalt brave the perils of death.

With a view to instruct men, I assumed the form of the slave, I who am their Lord and their God.

In order to heal their wounds, I have borne their infirmities, I have delivered into their hands My flesh and My blood, that My flesh might serve unto them as nourishment, and My blood be as beverage.

So as to destroy all iniquity within them, to unite them to My Father, and to unite them amongst themselves, there was no labour that I refused to endure.

I willed that My eyes should be a fountain of tears, and that sorrow should abide within My soul, and I consummated My sacrifice in embracing My cross.

Of thee I demand but this alone, that thou shouldst love those whom I so loved.

There are men who do not know thy heavenly Father, and who will not hear His voice, now, I say unto thee, if thou dost truly love, thou shalt manifest unto these men the patience of the Father, by thy patience towards them.

Reproach them not that they no longer see that which they saw in other days, or that they no longer hear those things they were wont to hear.

If thou thyself still hearest and seest, it is a gift thou hast received, it is a talent which is confided unto thee; wherefore then shouldst thou glory in it?

And if thou mayest not glory in this, wherefore shouldst thou treat with impatience those whom thy heavenly Father has not equally favoured?

Thou hast preserved the clear vision of truth, this vision do thou impart to thy brothers, who have ceased to enjoy it.

This labour is arduous, inasmuch as all souls are not alike, some unfold quickly to the rays of the light, whilst others shun these rays, because they dread to be enlightened, and others, again, abuse the light, saying within themselves: "The light will but convince us of sin, therefore, let us return to our darkness."

Now I say unto thee, even as thy heavenly Father speaks to those souls, and never grows wearied, even as He invites and awaits them, even so shalt thou unceasingly invite and await them.

The husbandman who sows his ground to-day shall not reap the fruits of his toil by to-morrow.

The days and the nights must pass over the soil which fosters the germs of the wheat, and when the days and the nights will have passed, the stalk shall have sprung up, and the ear shall have ripened.

And are not souls like the fields which thou sowest; therefore await not the harvest before the hour.

Preserve thy heart in patience, encompass these souls with thy tenderness, as the husbandman tends his ground with care and solicitude; and in so doing the germ of truth shall fructify within them and thy joy shall be immense.

II.

The Master.—My son, the truth is quickly effaced from the memory of men, it vanishes, as does the light of the day before the shades of the night.

And this is why I shall speak on with thee, lest the breath of the passions should sweep away from thy heart the seeds which I came to deposit within it.

And this time I shall address thee in parables, for it is needful that thou shouldst know the greatness, the height, and the depth of the charity of thy Father who is in heaven.

My son, the kingdom of heaven is like to a householder, who went out early in the morning to hire labourers into his vineyard.

And when he had agreed with the labourers for a penny a day, he sent them into his vineyard.

And going out about the third hour, he saw others standing in the market place idle, and he said to them:

"Go you also into my vineyard, and I will give you what shall be just." And they went their way.

And again, he went out about the sixth hour, and the ninth hour, and did in like manner.

And about the eleventh hour he went out and found others standing, and he said to them: "Why stand you here all day idle?"

They said to him: "Because no man hath hired us." He saith to them: "Go you also into the vineyard."

And when evening was come, the lord of the vineyard said to his steward: "Call the labourers and pay them their hire, beginning from the last even to the first."

When, therefore, they were come who came

about the eleventh hour, they received every man a penny.

And receiving it, they murmured against the master of the house, saying : "Those last have worked but one hour, and thou hast made them equal to us, that have borne the burden of the day and the heats."

But he, answering, said to one of them : "Friend, I do thee no wrong, didst thou not agree with me for a penny? Take what is thine, and go thy way; I will also give to the last, even as to thee.

"Or is it not lawful for me to do what I will?

"Is thy eye evil because I am good?"

My son, every word proceeding from men is readily understood, but thus it is not with every word coming from God.

Thou shouldst not comprehend that which I have said unto thee, did I not bestow on thee the grace which enlightens, and did I not explain to thee Myself the truths thou hast heard.

Let thy heart be not troubled or sad, inasmuch as My grace is with thee, and the sense of My words shall be unfolded to thee.

The Lord of the vineyard represents My Father, and the vineyard Myself, for it is written that I am the Vine, and that My Father is the Lord of the vineyard.

The workmen, whom the Father summons to labour in His vineyard, are all mankind.

And, as a branch can produce no fruit if it remains not attached to the stem, even so men cannot produce fruits of justice and life, if they know Me not, or if they unite not with Me.

For it is written: "It is life eternal to know Thee, O true God, and to know Thy Son, whom Thou hast sent."

The Lord of the vineyard knows that men shall not have this life, forasmuch as their spirit is bowed to this earth, and they raise not their hearts on high.

And behold why He goes out to call them, and to solicit them to become as one with Me, by grace and by love.

He goes out at early dawn, and that early dawn is the time of childhood.

Conceived in iniquity, He finds them charged with His maledictions, and incapable by themselves of rising from the depths of their misery.

And behold how He gives them, in His liberality, the true life, the necessary prelude to a better existence; behold how He delivers them from iniquity, and how He gives them His love.

And thus regenerated, these men grow, as it were; but quickly the divine light that is within them sheds out a lustre less brilliant, and already they hear a voice announcing to them: "Yet a little while, yet a little while, and you shall be children of darkness."

And the darkness comes, and the lot of many has become worse than at first.

Then the Lord of the vineyard goes out at the third hour of the day, and this third hour is the age of early youth.

It is at this age that the faculties of men begin to unfold themselves, and behold how the Lord of the vineyard delivers them a second time from the shadow of death.

Behold how He nourishes them with His word, behold how He enkindles within their spirit the flames of true faith, which the first breath of vice had extinguished.

Behold how He reveals to them the highest of mysteries, the most exalted of virtues.

Touched by the sweet and tender voice of the heavenly Father, those men make an effort with themselves.

They go forth to work in His vineyard, yet they do not all maintain their vow.

Many, wearied of sustaining the oppressive heat of the day, relinquish their task, and seek a place where they may repose and remain idle.

And now, the householder, seeing them no longer occupied with His vineyard, is not weary of calling them and still inviting them.

He goes out at the sixth hour, and this sixth hour is the age of manhood.

This period is critical and dangerous, for even as the earth is heated by the fires of the noonday sun, even so at this age are souls abandoned to the fury of passion.

Already, the evil has taken deep root, for many have lost the calm of conscience, and cease to seek the regions of peace.

In order to bring them back, the heavenly Father sheds bitterness into their hearts, even as one empties out a cup of gall, but they prefer their sadness to joy in its purity.

He causes their path to be watered with tears, in permitting that their evil acts and desires should turn against them, but they hear not the voice of those tears.

And when the Father sees His patience thus despised, He extends it yet farther.

And He goes out a fourth time to invite these rebellious men.

He calls them at a more advanced age, He makes His voice heard at the ninth hour, but many, distracted by the interests of time, and absorbed in their worldly affairs, answer as do the guests invited to the marriage feast.

But the Heavenly Father will not as yet abandon these men, who have preferred their own interests to the care of His vineyard.

He goes out a last time, He summons them at the eleventh hour, and this hour is the advanced period of old age.

These men are overcome by the heat, they have but one breath of life still remaining, they can with difficulty put their hand to the plough, yet behold how they are accepted as the workmen who came at the first hour of the day.

And when the day's labour is ended, they receive the same reward as the first.

They have laboured but little, yet, they are recompensed with liberality.

It is thus, My son, that thy Heavenly Father is patient.

There are some who arrive the latest, and who receive the same reward as the first, inasmuch as those work oftentimes more in one hour than do those workmen who have risen at break of day.

Thou didst come at the first summons of the Master to work in the vineyard, but the heat of the day has benumbed thy members, faintness has overcome thy heart, and thou didst not undertake the task with love, but like unto a mercenary.

Thou didst look back in putting thy hand to the plough, and if fear did not come to give thee the beginning of wisdom, it may be that thou wouldst have remained idle.

And he who labours as the slave, can he be compared to him who works as a free man?

Truly, truly, do I say unto thee, do not elevate thyself above thy brothers because thou didst come at the first hour, and be not harsh in regard to those who have not obeyed the voice of the Master.

These may yet come at the eleventh hour, and they shall be recompensed as thou thyself.

These things I have said unto thee, that so thou mayest never despair of the salvation of thy brothers, and that thou mayest not say within the depths of thy heart: "That man shall die as he lived, that man is already condemned.'

Close not thy heart to those souls that resist the word of life, forasmuch as the heavenly Father loves them, and still seeks after them.

How great soever may be the iniquities with which

they are charged, yet, abandon them not, lest that abandonment should be a crime which shall fall on thee on the day of justice.

III.

The Disciple.—O, my Master! Thy word is a word of love; but my heart has rebelled, and has said: "Wherefore should God tolerate the impious, and wherefore should He always await them?

"Had His arm been raised above them, the just should not be tempted to abandon their ways, neither should they be seduced by the prosperity of the wicked, even as the little birds are fascinated by the eyes of the serpent.

"If His justice were to show itself, the army of the impious should not gain strength, neither should it inundate this world, as the rivers swelled by the melted snow overflow the land with their tumultuous waves.

"They should be dispersed as is the dust on the highway by the wind of the south, and their impure breath, O Lord, should cease to sully the souls that love Thee."

The Master.—My son, thy spirit is tardy in comprehending Me, because thou seest things but in a partial manner.

Thou hast not the capacity of beholding all at

one glance, thy sight can discern but one point of the horizon, and that is why thy heart revolts.

They who dwell in the depths of the valleys bounded by the high mountains, distinguish but one point of the heavens, and easily imagine that the universe is very small.

But thus it is not with those who travel from north to south, and who traverse all seas and all shores.

Those have a more just idea of creation, those feel a deeper admiration.

Thou seest but one point of My doctrine, and I would reveal it to thee in its entirety, for if I do not so reveal it, thou shalt rest with thine own spirit, and thy spirit is not Mine.

It is fitting that I should instruct thee, not alone by words, but still more by example, for men do not understand aright, neither do they rightly perform other things save those they have witnessed.

Did I make known unto thee the actions of the Son of Man, thy heart would remain insensible, and thou wouldst not seek to imitate them.

My son, may My grace be with thee, and do thou listen.

The time being come when I was to be removed from this world, I resolved to repair to Jerusalem.

And I sent before Me people to announce My coming into those places through which I was to pass.

They set out, and entered a city of Samaria, in order to prepare for Me all that was needful, but the people would not receive Me, as believing that I was proceeding to Jerusalem.

My disciples, James and John, seeing this, could not suffer the affront offered to their Master, and, addressing Me, they exclaimed:

"Lord, dost Thou not will that we should command the fire of heaven to descend upon them and consume them?"

I then turned to them, and reprimanded them in these words: You know not of what spirit you are.

The Son of Man is not come to lose souls, but to save them.

Now, My son, even as I condemned on that day the zeal of My disciples, so likewise at this hour do I condemn thine.

When thy heart rebels against the patience of thy heavenly Father, who does not pour down His wrath on the evil, neither dost thou know of what spirit thou art.

Thou believest thou hast My spirit, because thou wouldst avenge Me for the outrages of the impious, and wouldst spare the good in separating them from the evil doers.

But I say unto thee, truly, that spirit that animates thee is a spirit of vengeance and harshness. Do thou learn of Me to be meek and humble of heart.

When My disciples would chastise the inhabitants of Samaria, it was because they remembered that Elias had called down the fires of heaven on the armed force that a king had sent out to apprehend him.

And knowing that I was greater than Elias, they believed that for that reason My indignation should fall on those who would not receive Me, and that the might of My arm should crush them.

But My law is not as was the ancient law, it admits not that men should demand an eye for an eye, or a tooth for a tooth; My law is a law of grace and of love.

My spirit is a spirit of meekness, and they who would be My disciples should not call down the chastisements of My Father on those who wander astray.

My spirit is a spirit of patience, and they who would follow Me should not yield to anger or violence, as the lion of the desert when wounded by the arrow of the huntsman.

My spirit is a spirit of charity, and they who love Me should love as I have loved.

Now, he who loves like Me suffers not hatred to penetrate his heart, or the thirst of vengeance to consume his soul.

Thou demandest that the fires of heaven should descend on the guilty, because thou fearest lest the just be seduced.

And dost thou not know that the grace of thy Father in heaven is all-powerful?

For thy Father is faithful, and will not permit the children of men to be tempted beyond their strength; and if they be tempted, He will afford them aid against the temptation.

The spirit of evil is powerless against the true just, for, "He that dwelleth in the aid of the Most High, shall abide under the protection of the God of heaven.

"He shall say to the Lord: Thou art my protector and my refuge: my God, in Him will I trust.

"For He hath delivered me from the snare of the hunter, and from the sharp word.

"He will overshadow thee with His shoulders, and under His wings thou shalt trust.

"His truth shall compass thee with a shield, thou shalt not be afraid of the terror of the night.

"Of the arrow that flieth in the day, of the business that walketh in the dark, of rain, or of the noonday devil.

"A thousand shall fall at thy side, and ten thousand at thy right hand, but it shall not come nigh thee.

"For He hath given His angels charge over thee, to keep thee in all thy ways.

"In their hands they shall bear thee up, lest thou dash thy foot against a stone.

"Thou shalt walk upon the asp and the basilisk, and thou shalt trample underfoot the lion and the dragon.

"Because he hath hoped in Me, I will deliver him: I will protect him, because he hath known My name.

"He shall cry to Me, and I will hear him: I am with him in his trouble.

"I will deliver him, and I will glorify him; I will fill him with length of days, and I will show him My salvation."

Therefore, fear not thou for the just, who place their confidence in the Most High; they alone are lost who wish to perish, for it is written: "Peace to men of good will."

These endure persecution from the evil, but dost thou not know that it is further written: "Blessed are they who suffer persecution for justice sake, for theirs is the kingdom of heaven"?

He who has not suffered, what does he know? As gold is purified by the fire, even so do virtues become developed in suffering.

My son, did I not endure persecution for thee, and for all men; and My words, were they not treated as blasphemies?

Wherefore should I have traversed that mournful path, if thou wouldst not traverse it in thy turn? Love the cross, but do thou likewise love those who inflict it.

Thou callest down weighty chastisements on the wicked, lest their army should increase and become masters of this world.

But dost thou not know that chastisements instruct not the men of iniquity?

For does not the black and dense vapour arising from their hearts, calcined by the consuming fire of the passions, does not that vapour cast a cloud over their eyeballs?

At each step they succumb, and they know not where they fall.

Chastisements at times rouse from their sleep of death those whom they strike, but those others, who are only spectators, become hardened and continue unmoved.

They are unshaken, because in the pride of their hearts they have said within themselves, "Chance would have it thus."

And, as not knowing how to distinguish the finger of the Almighty, they change not their ways, and their hideous laughter fascinates and bears away those who have not placed all their faith in the Most High.

Say not, therefore: "If the Almighty would lend me the strength of His arm, I should annihilate those who blaspheme against His name, I should pursue with a rod of iron those who observe not His law."

Truly, do I say unto thee, hold not this language, for so thy zeal would be guilty, and thou shouldst lose My spirit, which is a spirit of love.

Thy heavenly Father does not display His power, He breaks not these vessels of clay that hold but filth and corruption, because He wills that all justice be consummated.

And to this end He rewards in the wicked that little of good that is mingled with their iniquities, in sparing them in this life from the fire of His anger.

Thy heavenly Father does not hasten to chastise,

because eternity is in His hands, and because He wills that all mercy be consummated.

And, therefore, He would still wait for the impious till the approach of the eleventh hour; for I say unto thee, that same hour shall be an hour of salvation to many.

My son, let thy heart cease to revolt against My words; although thou standest at this present moment, yet thou mayest fall, and there is not one sin against heaven that men have committed which another man may not perpetrate.

And as thou wouldst not wish others to call down the fire of heaven on thee if fallen thyself, so do thou not imprecate the vengeance of God on the children of darkness.

Do thou unceasingly invoke for them the divine mercy and grace, this being My true spirit; for, I repeat unto thee, I am meek and humble of heart.

All souls are precious in My eyes, consequently do thou love them; the Son of Man did not come to lose them, but to save them.

IV.

The Disciple.—O Master! my heart clings to Thy doctrine as the ivy to the habitations of men, and already I feel that Thou hast awoke within me a new zeal.

Before I heard Thy word I was sad, because

my eyes did not distinguish how I might establish harmony amongst souls.

I contemplated their dispersion with anguish, and I discovered not its true cause; then did my arms fall down with lassitude, and I relinquished my task.

This day Thou hast consoled and strengthened my heart, because Thou hast revealed to me Thy spirit, and the immensity of Thy charity.

And so I shall not quit this living world before I shall have afforded to some souls the joys of that union that passes from this earth to the heights of the heavens.

And, behold how I shall make men love the truth which brings with it salvation and peace; behold how they shall believe in Thee, forasmuch as my word shall cease to be fruitless and harsh.

Lord, it shall be full of Thy meekness and charity, and they shall hear Thy doctrine, and they shall find it sweeter than milk or than honey.

O Master! complete Thy work, teach Thy servant to walk in Thy ways, for if Thou wilt not show him all the paths of love, his soul shall faint on the way.

The spirit of patience shall fly from him, even as the birds of the warm regions abandon the valleys of the north at the approach of the first cold.

O Master! Thou hast said to me, that we should love mankind, lay open to me this day the secrets of the science of meekness, and let Thy word instruct me in the obligations of true love.

The Master.—My son, it is not flesh and blood which have made thee understand that thy heart should open to mercy; but it is My Father who is in heaven.

This is why I shall hear thy prayer; and, behold, thou shalt learn the obligations of the true love.

It has been said of the Son of Man: "Behold My servant, I will uphold Him; My elect, My soul delighteth in Him; I have given My Spirit upon Him; He shall bring forth judgment to the Gentiles.

"He shall not cry, nor have respect to persons, neither shall His voice be heard abroad.

"The bruised reed He shall not break, and smoking flax He shall not quench; He shall bring forth judgment unto truth.

"He shall not be sad nor troublesome."

And now, My son, that which the prophets wrote concerning the Son of Man, I, who am greater than all the prophets, I, who am the Son of Man, this same do I announce concerning those who love.

Truly, do I say unto thee, he who loves, cries not aloud, neither does he make exception of persons.

There are some who say, "If our voice become not terrible, like unto that of the thunder, the wicked will not understand, O Lord, the rigour of Thy justice, they shall remain in their indifference, they shall sleep a sleep of death till the day of Thy judgment.

And, again, there are men who say, "We have spoken, and meekness has not ceased to accompany our words.

"But those who listened to us shook their heads, and mocked us; but let us now speak the words which resound afar, and which echo like the voice of the storm that precedes the tempest."

Such is the language held by men, but I say unto thee, truly, the virtue of the word which touches and which converts hearts, that virtue dwells not in the force of thy voice, but in the strength of My grace.

For this divine force, is it not all-powerful, and, in its sweetness, does it not break the cedars of Lebanon?

Wherefore wouldst thou assign to My grace a force wholly human, for that which thou stylest human power, is it not weakness and impotence?

It is requisite that My word should penetrate hearts, even as the water penetrates the earth; and how should it penetrate them, if thou wouldst change it in robbing it of its divine tenderness?

Do not men feel themselves agreeably attracted by the warbling of the birds, and are they not violently repelled by the hissing of the serpent?

Dost thou desire to love souls and to save them, do not then terrify them, nor let them hear the din of thy voice echo afar.

The clamour and the loud sounds that strike upon the ears of the traveller at the dead of the night trouble him, and render him incapable of avoiding the danger that approaches.

And the souls thou wouldst save through love, are they not, as it were, immersed in the midst of thick darkness?

And if thy word were to reach them as the sharp cry of the fierce beasts of the forest, should they not be appalled, and in their terror take flight?

And should not that flight be to them as a second abyss still deeper than the first?

Till now, thou hast spoken much, but thy words have been fruitless, because thou hast not reposed thy reliance on Me.

Thou didst too much confide in the eloquence of human wisdom; in thy folly thou didst believe that this would prove as a lever to move the world of souls, and behold, why thy words remained fruitless.

To the children of earth leave the measures of violence, their works are of this earth, consequently, those means are most fitting.

Do not thou adopt them, for thy work is the work of heaven.

All words coming from God have attraction; and, therefore, thou shouldst bear them to guilty souls in all the force of their sweetness, else they shall be no longer the words which attract, but those which repulse and which kill.

Raise not thy voice in such a way as that those who walk in the paths of iniquity, stunned by its clamours, should fly from thy presence.

And if they should fly, who shall then speak to them? And if no one should exhort them, will not the life that comes from on high be extinguished within them?

And, behold, how the genius of evil shall uproot their last remnant of faith, how he shall wrest from them the very instinct of their destination.

And, behold, how he shall destroy all bonds and all love, behold how he shall bend them to the earth, how he shall knead them as mud, how he shall stifle them in their own abominations.

Arise, then, speak to the wicked, lest they should reproach thee with thy silence on that day when I shall come to judge this world, but let thy words not wound them, or scare them from the ways of justice.

Some shall reply to the sweetness of thy voice with the ghastly smile of the spirit of darkness, for their flesh has already felt the impure contact of the spectres of the abyss, but let not the blame of their revolt be laid to thy charge.

Be thou not wearied, nor let joy abandon thee, for there are few who thus resist till their latest day.

My son, do thou assume the courage of thy love, and if thou hast it not, demand it of My Father, who is likewise thy Father, and My Father will grant it thee.

And when thou shalt have received it, do thou preserve it within thy heart; for, truly I say unto thee, if thou wilt not thus preserve it, the wicked will fly from thee, and they shall thus remain in isolation.

For thou hast read that which is written: "Woe unto him who is alone."

V.

The Prophet had announced of the Son of Man that He would not crush the bruised reed, neither would He extinguish the smoking torch; now I predict the like things concerning those who love.

O My son, do thou beware of believing that evil can ever invade the souls of men, so as to wrest from them all goodness and all aspirations after good.

There are some who have strayed away from thy heavenly Father, because, in their inordinate love of self, they believed they were like unto Him in whose presence the universe is as if it were not.

And behold how they have contemned the revelations and the lessons coming from on high, behold how they have said in their insensate rage: "We shall not serve."

There are others who have not erred by the pride of the spirit, or by confidence in their own reason, but by the weakness of their hearts.

And behold how those have stopped in their course, saying within themselves: "We are tired of the strife, our force deserts us, the day is advanced, the sun has already darted his last rays, and let us repose our wearied limbs.

And they have corrupted their ways.

The flesh had triumphed over the spirit, and when they awoke from their sleep defeat had given their souls a disrelish of the struggle.

And now these men have lost all worth; but is there nought remaining within their souls which may be styled human virtue? No, do thou not judge them thus harshly.

They all continue to practise some good, and if thou couldst search the loins and the hearts of men, thou shouldst discover in their lives both actions and thoughts worthy of praise.

And who has told thee that these thoughts and these actions shall not be recompensed by some graces which shall dispel their darkness, and which shall turn them aside from the ways that lead to perdition?

And there are others in whom evil has made still greater havoc; it has, as it would seem, even superabounded within them, so that their spirit and their flesh are now no longer but, as it were, a spirit and a flesh of sin.

But I say unto thee, do thou beware of believing that these last have lost all goodness, or that they have crushed within their souls all generous impulse.

In these men is there not remaining that which the hand of God had placed within them?

They have sullied the divine work, but they

have not annihilated it; and if they have not wholly destroyed it, have they not still left within them some remnant of good?

And if there yet exist within them a something of good which they may not eradicate, forasmuch as all power is not given them,—wherefore, then, should they not be treated as the bruised reeds which there is a possibility of straightening, or like the smoking torch which may once more be rekindled?

When thine eyes rest on the waters of the ocean, thou seest nought save a barren field of waves, yet there dwells on the bed of those waters a vast harvest of invisible plants.

And these, after a brief space, thou shalt see rise above its depths, and become expanded on its surface.

As thy heavenly Father has strewed over the bed of the waters these invisible plants, has He not in like manner deposited at the root of evil the germ of good? And, after a little while, that germ shall likewise unfold itself.

And what matters it if thine eyes of flesh cannot discern it? For does it not suffice that thou knowest its existence?

Be sure, therefore, where thou dost tread, and walk not inconsiderately over the field of the householder, lest thou shouldst stifle the precious germs that are therein deposited, in thy precipitation and imprudence.

Thou shouldst demand little of him who cannot bestow much, because, if thou askest of him more than he can bestow, his heart will be troubled, and seeing himself unable to satisfy thee, he will give nothing whatever.

Does the mother demand of her new-born babe to partake of a solid nutriment? Or does the planter cut down the tender shrub because it bears no fruit?

And art thou not in the field of the Father, art thou not as a mother and as a planter?

Therefore, when thou mayest encounter men like unto bruised reeds, as no longer having that life that comes from on high, do thou not ask of them directly that which they cannot well give.

Or, is faith extinguished within their hearts? Do thou commence by imploring them to elevate themselves to God by prayer.

It is not through reasonings thou mayest convince them, faith being a heavenly gift, in order to obtain it one must needs solicit for it.

And if thou shouldst succeed in persuading these men to pray, do thou console thyself, and let thy soul be in joy; for thou hast read that which is written: "Ask, and you shall receive, knock, and it shall be opened unto you."

Yet, be guarded of requiring from them long prayers, for they would not willingly recite them, or else they would recite them ill.

And if thus it happened, should not discouragement take hold of their souls, and should not their state be worse than at first?"

Are not they who are sick in spirit like to those who are sick in body?

And if these latter cannot support the abundant and solid nutriment of the healthy, can the first easily undertake the labour of those who have not abandoned the ways of justice?

Truly, do I say unto thee, apply thyself rather to persuade how it is fitting to pray than to require long hours of prayer.

A short aspiration, when coming from a contrite and humble heart, does it not suffice in order to attract the most signal of graces?

It is not a multiplicity of words that rises with an odour of suavity to the throne of the King of glory, but it is that fervour that accompanies them.

These things I have not said unto thee so as to cool thine ardour, but so as that thy zeal may not be imprudent.

Do thou diffuse the truth over those souls which are removed from God, but diffuse it drop by drop; they are as yet too feeble to be enabled to support it in its plenitude.

And, when the truth shall have entirely penetrated them, do thou then demand good works; and, enlightened by the light coming from on high, and strengthened by the divine gift, they shall no longer take umbrage at thy words.

Nevertheless, let thy words be always full of tenderness; for if men easily understand the truth, yet they will not practise it without much effort.

Virtue means to say—force, and the children of men being weak, the struggle against self casts them into gloom, and when sadness once visits them, they are nigh to a fall.

And, should they happen to fall, do thou not discourage them, but seek to raise them with mildness and sweetness; and even should they succumb several times, do thou not reproach them too loudly with their fall.

He who falls after long struggles is not as guilty in the eyes of My Father as thou mayest suppose.

Be then satisfied with the least efforts of those souls which thou lovest, and make known thy contentment unto them.

There shall be a deep sorrow within thee that thy efforts are not always crowned with success, yet suffer not that sorrow to appear too much exteriorly.

It might be that thy sadness would stifle that good which has been already effected; and it is a vast advantage for a soul to have begun to struggle.

O, My son! do thou come in aid by thy joy to those who seek the kingdom of God and His justice, for, truly I say unto thee, these are already the friends of My Father.

VI.

The Disciple.—O Master, till now I have listened with too much confidence to the lessons of men, and behold why the doctrine Thou teachest me seems to me as it were a new doctrine.

Thou hast dilated my heart, but my spirit is not as yet reassured; it hesitates to enter into the ways of love which Thou hast pointed out, forasmuch as it has said: "This love, is it not weakness? and weakness, is it not the enemy of souls?"

O Master, place before my eyes Thine example, and that will dissipate my doubts and uncertainties.

I have need to know how Thou didst complete that which the prophets announced concerning Thee, and what have been the fruits of Thy divine tenderness.

Thou hast already said to me that men alone perform well that which they have seen others do, then do Thou teach me what Thou didst do at the time of Thy appearance on earth.

Then I shall no longer hesitate, and, strengthened by the divine light of Thy works, I shall rise as a giant, so as to run in Thy ways.

The Master.—I shall not refuse to thy spirit the light thou demandest, but, first, I would once more speak with thee concerning My Father.

The Father and I are but One, it is consequently

needful that I should further reveal to thee Him who sent Me, for then thou shalt better understand the works of Him who was sent.

A certain man had two sons, and the younger said to his father: "My father, give me the portion of substance that falleth to me." And he divided unto them his substance.

And not many days after, the younger son, gathering all together, went to a far country, and there wasted all his patrimony with living riotously.

And after he had spent all, there came a mighty famine in that country, and he began to be in want.

And he went and cleaved to one of the citizens of that country, and he sent him into his farm to feed swine.

And he would fain have filled himself with the husks the swine did eat, and no man gave unto him.

And returning to himself, he said: "How many hired servants in my father's house abound with bread, and I here perish with hunger?

"I will arise, and will go to my father, and say to him: Father, I have sinned against heaven and before thee, I am not worthy to be called thy son; make me as one of thy hired servants."

And, rising up, he came to his father; and when he was yet a great way off, his father saw him, and was moved with compassion, and, running to him, fell upon his neck and kissed him.

And the son said to him: "Father, I have

sinned against heaven, and before thee; I am not worthy to be called thy son."

But the father said to his servants: "Bring forth quickly the first robe, and put it on him, and put a ring on his hand, and shoes on his feet; and bring hither the fatted calf, and kill it, and let us eat and make merry; because this my son was dead, and is now come to life, was lost, and is found." And they began to make merry.

Now the eldest son was in the field, and when he came and drew nigh to the house, he heard music and dancing, and he called one of the servants, and asked what these things meant.

And he said to him: "Thy brother is come, and thy father hath killed the fatted calf because he hath received him safe."

And he was angry, and would not go in. His father, therefore, coming out, began to entreat him.

And he, answering, said to his father: "Behold for so many years do I serve thee, and I have never transgressed thy commandments, and yet thou hast never given me a kid to make merry with my friends; but as soon as this thy son is come, thou hast killed for him the fatted calf."

But he said to him: "Son, thou art always with me, and all I have is thine.

"But it was fit we should make merry, and be glad; for this thy brother was dead, and is come to life again, he was lost, and is found."

O, My son, when thy heart was sad, thou

didst come to Me, and thou didst say: "My Master."

I would truly be thy Master, and this is why I shall expound to thee the sense of that word thou hast just now heard.

That Man who had two sons, is thy heavenly Father, and those two represent the good and the evil.

In the elder are represented the just, or such as believe themselves to be, or boast of being, such, like to the Scribes and the Pharisees.

In the younger are represented the public sinners, with whom the Son of Man eat and conversed.

Now do I say unto thee, even as did the younger, so acts the man who abandons himself to iniquity.

Tired of living in obedience to the authority of the heavenly Father, he removes to a distance, and seeks to renounce His authority.

He has received his patrimony, which means the substance given to all creatures, and he goes afar to dissipate this precious substance.

Now, thou knowest in what consists this patrimony; it is that grace that strengthens in the combat, which consoles in tribulation; it is reason, which distinguishes good from evil, the just from the unjust, and the true from the false.

This substance is the heart, the home of love, by which the finite unites itself in intimate union with the infinite.

This substance is that liberty by which the

children of men may choose that which pleases them, or may elevate or abase themselves accordingly as they may choose virtue or vice.

That substance is the body, that living tabernacle of the immortal soul, her companion, and the co-heir of her eternal destinies.

And now, how acts the man of sin? He dissipates that glorious substance.

He has estranged himself from the Father, and, behold how he no longer possesses that grace which consoles and which fortifies.

And, behold how darkness has enveloped his reason, behold how his heart has lost all its love.

Justice abode within him, and now there remains nought save crime, the beauty of his silver has changed into mud, and the strength of his wine has degenerated into the weakness of water.

And, after the man of sin has thus squandered his substance, behold how his heart within him is sad, for he has already felt the might of the evil one crushing him down, as the hand of a cruel master crushes his slave.

And, in the bitterness of his soul he has said within himself: "I shall arise, and I shall go to my Father;" and he arises, and he sets out; and, so soon as his Father perceives him returning to Him, this good Father goes out to meet and embrace him.

He was covered with miserable rags, and now he is attired in the robe of innocence.

He was dying of hunger, he disputed his nourishment with the unclean beasts, but he is admitted to the festivity, for, behold, My flesh is bestowed on him as food, and My blood is given him as drink.

In truth, I say unto thee, it is thus that the Almighty loves souls, and yet, there are some who rebel against this love.

There are some who have not abandoned the right way, and who have not squandered their substance; and these men rebel, exclaiming, "Lord, we have served Thee during many years, without having ever despised Thy commandments, nevertheless, Thou hast never shown towards us all that love; but this other son of Thine is scarce returned when Thou heapest him with favours."

And, does not My Father reply to these jealous souls in these terms: "You are always with Me, and all I possess is yours, but, there is cause for rejoicing, because this your brother was dead, and he is restored to life, he was lost, and he is found."

Consequently, do thou beware of prescribing bounds to the tenderness of thy heavenly Father, and be not jealous of that which He testifies towards those who return to Him.

There are some, who, in seeing sinners brought back to the right path by means of affliction, say within themselves, if their prosperity had not abandoned them, they should not have left their evil ways, and so they are harsh in regard to these men.

Now, I say unto thee, they who hold this language love not their brothers.

For, did not the prodigal, in order to re-enter the bosom of his family, did he not wait till misery and suffering had become his portion?

Believe not thou that the conversion is faulty which is the fruit of tears.

My Father has in the treasures of His love graces of every species, and grief is oftentimes one of the most signal which He grants to His rebellious children.

There are others who easily doubt of their brothers, and say within themselves: "If we do not recall to them forcibly the enormity of their past wanderings, they will avail themselves of our indulgence to fall back into the disorders of their hearts.

And, behold the reason why they will not manifest to them a holy joy.

Now, I tell thee, he who loves, doubts not thus hastily of his brother; he rejoices at the good which he witnesses; and his soul, which has placed all its hope in the Lord, regards the future with confidence.

Does thy heavenly Father count thus rigorously with the children of men? For did He not cut short the discourse of the prodigal with a kiss, and that kiss, was it not the kiss of peace?

There are others, in fine, who dread to show themselves over-eager, or tender towards those of their brothers who begin to weep for their failings.

And those say within themselves: "Let this our joy be interior, let it not be too much displayed outwardly, for the just would be scandalized thereat."

But I say unto thee in truth, dread not this scandal; woe to those who take alarm at thy joy, forasmuch as thy joy is holy.

Did not the father of the prodigal know that his son would take umbrage at his tenderness?

And did he not know that this his tenderness would be reproached to him, and that his joy would be blamed?

Thou didst hear his reply: "It is fitting to rejoice, inasmuch as thy brother was dead, and he is restored to life; he was lost, and he is found."

Therefore, let not the judgments of men impede the impulse of thy heart, for thy heart is free, and to God alone it belongs to say to it: No further shalt thou go.

VII.

The Master.—In order to speak to thee of My Father, I have placed on My lips words which men understand, and, behold, why many things are yet hidden from thine eyes.

What is all the eloquence of the children of this earth in essaying to render the celestial harmonies of divine love?

Consequently, do thou not believe that the love of My father has been here portrayed in all its plenitude.

Or else, thou shouldst take a drop of dew for the immensity of the waters of the ocean, and a faint flambeau for the sun in his meridian heat.

In that figure which already touches thy heart and penetrates thy soul, thou hast discovered but a particle of the goodness of My Father, and this particle is the smallest of all.

Thine eyes have seen that love which receives and which pardons, but they have not as yet discovered that other which searches and anticipates.

The hour is nigh when I shall speak to thee of this love, but before that hour comes I must needs hearken to thy prayer.

Thou hast said unto Me, "O Master! display unto me the divine light of Thy works, and my spirit within me reassured, shall no longer hesitate."

Let it be done unto thee according to thy word, and let this light be bestowed upon thee.

O My son, may My grace be with thee, and do thou listen to Me.

A Pharisee having invited Me to eat with him at his house, I repaired thither and placed Myself at table.

Now, there was in the city a sinful woman, who, having learned that I was to eat at the house of a Pharisee, brought with her an alabaster vase full of precious ointment.

And resting behind Me, she prostrated herself

at My feet, she bathed them with her tears, and she dried them with her hair, she kissed them, and perfumed them with the balm she carried with her.

The Pharisee who had invited Me, seeing all this, said within himself: "If this Man were a prophet, He would know that this woman who draws nigh to Him is a sinner."

And I, answering, said to him: "Simon, I have somewhat to say to thee." And he said, "Master, say it."

"A certain creditor had two debtors, the one owed him five hundred pence, and the other fifty.

"And, whereas they had not wherewith to pay, he forgave them both. Which therefore of the two loveth him most?"

Simon, answering, said: "I suppose that he to whom he forgave most."

And I said to him: "Thou hast judged rightly." And turning to the woman, I said unto Simon: "Dost thou see this woman? I entered into thy house, thou gavest Me no water for My feet, but she, with her tears, hath washed My feet, and with her hairs hath wiped them.

"Thou gavest Me no kiss, but she, since she came in, hath not ceased to kiss My feet.

"My head with oil thou didst not anoint, but she with ointment hath anointed My feet.

"Wherefore I say to thee: Many sins are forgiven her, because she hath loved much, but to whom less is forgiven, he loveth less."

And I said to her: "Thy sins are forgiven thee." And they that sat at meat with Me, began to say within themselves: "Who is this that forgiveth sins also?"

And I said to the woman: "Thy faith hath made thee safe, go in peace."

And thus, My son, did I fulfil that which the prophet had announced concerning Me, and thus it was that I did not break the bruised reed, nor extinguish the smoking torch.

Thou dost behold this woman; her hands are impure, her lips are sullied, the honour of her name is lost, and when men encounter her, they say within themselves, "She is the public sinner of the city."

And, lo! that woman felt within the depths of her heart, as it were, a something which kindled within her, and that was a feeling of love.

Now, love gives confidence, and confidence is a commencement of wisdom.

And, impelled by that confidence, she arises, pierces the crowd, and prostrates herself at My feet.

And how did I act in presence of that woman? Did My eyes light up with a holy indignation? Did I repulse her as she approached Me?

Or did I fear that My sanctity should be profaned by the perfumed essences with which she sprinkled My feet, and .by the contact of the tresses of her hair with which she wiped them?

And did I not read into the soul of Simon?

And that which I read, was it not harshness and contempt?

And if he blamed Me not for the welcome with which I greeted the sinner, was it not because there arose within his spirit an impious thought, and because he said within himself: "If that Man were a prophet He should necessarily know who is she who draws nigh to Him, and what she is, for she is a sinner."

And seeing this, I endured the judgments of the Pharisee, for it was preferable to endure these than not to receive with love the sorrow of that woman.

Had I sought the esteem of Simon, My countenance would have grown severe, and the sinner should have returned to her evil ways; and her heart, which had opened itself to love, should have hardened for evermore.

But because I despised unjust judgments, behold how I restored sight to her who could see no longer.

O My son, let prudence guide thy steps, yet be thou prudent with sobriety.

One should not brave the judgments of men, because in so doing one may do much evil, neither should one be their slave, for I say unto thee in truth, he who falls into this servitude, oftentimes does even more evil.

Perhaps thou mayest say within thyself: "If I receive under the shadow of my tent those who have sullied their hands, and lost their honour, what shall become of me?

"The just shall blame me, and afterwards they shall accuse me of sin."

Thou shalt perhaps say within thyself: "If I should accept of gifts from the hands of the wicked, these gifts shall be turned against me, whereas the just shall say to each other: 'They who thus communicate with the impious shall not be worthy to live with us;' and the just shall desert the threshold of my dwelling."

But, I say, woe to him who has given entrance to servile fear into his heart. That fear shall crush all love within him.

He shall do much evil, because he shall seek his own advantage before all other things. He shall arrest in their onward career those who had already advanced in the ways of justice.

And dost thou not know that men only judge by appearances, and that many of them are deceived by appearances.

And frequently, they style men of iniquity those in whom justice abides, and whom the grace of My Father has already purified.

That woman who came to pour out her perfumes on My head, and to water My feet with the tears of her sorrow, that woman was no longer a sinner in that hour when she performed these acts.

Betwixt her and evil there was a distance which the finger of God alone could measure; and yet, contempt and ignominy still attended her steps.

And how many souls come to thee broken and crushed in the eyes of men, but which are no longer broken or crushed in those of thy heavenly Father?

Fear not thou to receive them, when they seek in thee solace and support.

Be careful not to assume a look of severity which might scare them away, for truly I say unto thee, when thou believest thou dost repulse a sinner thou dost oftentimes repulse the just.

And now, wherefore shouldst thou not have on thy lips some words which may dilate the heart and raise the courage of those who, wearied of living in the chilly and dismal regions of vice, seem to desire the land which is the abode of peace.

They advance towards good, but their course is long and difficult, and it is for thee to accelerate their march.

And the word which shall come to extol their first efforts, shall it not be a word fruitful and blessed?

Behold in what manner I rendered testimony to the sinner.

"Simon, Simon," I said, "dost thou see this woman? I entered into thy house, thou gavest Me no water for My feet, but she, with her tears hath washed My feet, and with her hairs hath wiped them.

"Thou gavest Me no kiss, but she, since she came in, hath not ceased to kiss My feet.

"My head with oil thou didst not anoint, but she with ointment hath anointed My feet."

And when that woman had heard those words, thou didst see how she was consoled in her sorrow, and how she was confirmed in the holy desires of her soul.

And having thus augmented within her the gift of faith, I completed My work, and I said unto her: "Many sins are forgiven to her that has loved much; go in peace, thy faith has saved thee."

If thou didst imitate the Son of Man, how many souls should be aided in their first steps?

And when thou shouldst have aided them, couldst thou not then accomplish thy task, and say unto them:

"Fear not you, the spirit of love has descended into you, He has covered you with His shadow, a divine mystery has been accomplished which has astonished the heavens; and that mystery is one of pardon."

Till now thou hast not comprehended that heart should be won by heart, and that is why a vast number of souls who came to thee have fled away from thee.

And now, that thine eyes have seen the light of My works, do thou learn to despise the judgments that separate the just from the sinners.

The grace of My Father has always its hour for these latter, and when that hour shall come, do thou remember Me.

SIXTH COLLOQUY.

THE DISCIPLE HAS DONE AS THE MASTER HAD COUNSELLED HIM, BUT THE PEOPLE OF SOULS HAS NOT LISTENED TO HIM, AND HE IS SAD.—THE MASTER REPLIES TO HIM THAT TILL THIS MOMENT HE HAS HAD WITHIN HIS HEART NO LOVE SAVE THAT WHICH RECEIVES, BUT THAT THE HOUR IS COME WHEN HE SHALL TEACH HIM A NEW LOVE.

THIS LOVE IS THAT WHICH PURSUES AND WHICH SEEKS.

THE DISCIPLE DEMANDS OF THE MASTER BY WHAT MEANS HE MAY BRING BACK THE SOUL WHICH HAS GONE ASTRAY IN THE WAYS OF EVIL.

THE MASTER INSTRUCTS HIM HOW TO SPEAK, SHOWING HIM WHAT SHALL BE THE POWER OF HIS WORDS.

THE MASTER TEACHES ALL THESE THINGS BY HIS EXAMPLE.

SIXTH COLLOQUY.

I.

The Disciple.—O Master, behold me, I have walked in the ways which Thou hast taught me, I have acted in conformity to Thy word.

I have kept my patience, I have opened my heart to that love whose secrets Thou hast revealed unto me.

I have not imprecated the anger of God on the heads of the children of darkness, I have not cried aloud; and when the bruised reed stood before me, I have not broken it.

And my heart is still sad. It is sad because few souls have come to me.

I have seen souls draw together and form themselves as it were into a great army, and those souls were as the waves stirred up by the wind of the north on the face of the deep.

And now, the billows do not rush towards that point where rages the wind; in their tumultuous march, they fly those regions from whence the tempest proceeds.

And since Thou didst speak to me, I did not arise upon the people of souls like to an impetuous wind. Love descended on me, and I felt, O Master, as it were, the touch of a something divine; and it was Thy spirit that came to strengthen me.

And now, how shall I act? Thou hast transformed me within the depths of my soul, and I have remained unfruitful.

Thou hast said that it was needful to love, and my heart has loved; and yet my brothers come not to me, they still disappear, they still go their ways.

Yet a little while, and I shall cease to see them.

O, Master! how shall I act? Must that love which Thou hast given me bear no fruits within me; save those of sorrow and solitude?

Or shall Thy servant seat himself upon the earth, as the ancients of the city of Sion, and remain in silence? Or shall he rest with his head bowed down, as the virgins of Jerusalem?

O Master, I shall raise my eyes unto Thee, even as the prophet raised his eyes towards the high places, whence succour came unto him.

Do Thou open mine eyelids that I may see, and that my sterility may be vanquished by the holy vision of Thy light.

The Master.—Let thy heart, O My son, be not as a barren soil, for behold how I shall render it fruitful.

Till now, thou hast learned from Me nought

save the power of the love which receives; now, I say unto thee, that power is great, yet, it is incomplete.

Many are the souls which it may not reach, forasmuch as these souls escape it, and they escape because they do not know it.

The hour is now come wherein I shall reveal unto thee a new love; and that love is the one which pursues and which searches.

It is written that no one should place his light under a bushel, but I say unto thee: Neither do thou hold captive the holy flame of love I have lighted within thee.

That flame must needs be active, and it must pervade the world of souls, as the lightning flits athwart the heavenly arch.

In the depths of the night of storm, till the lightning has glimmered out, all nature lies plunged in dense shadow.

One man seeks another, and finds him not, the fox seeks his den, and neither does he find it.

Yet, let the lightning but gleam forth, and men shall distinguish each other, and the fox shall find his den, whereas that fire that pierces the clouds has darted athwart the shades of the forests, and its brightness has penetrated the darkest retreats.

My son, the souls of men flee far from thee; they flee from each other, because in traversing this world, they traverse it in darkness.

They see not thy love which awaits them, consequently, thy love must not linger in the place of its rest.

Let it dart forth its light, let it shed it abroad on the heights of the mountains, and through the narrow dells, and from sea to sea, and from east to west.

And, let that light not grow weary in its course, and then shall the souls receive a vision of love that shall save them, and they shall unfold before that vision as the leaves of the flowers open to the rays of the sun of noon.

The Disciple.—O Master! after what manner may my love become visible, and how may I impart unto souls the vision that shall save them?

Is my heart like the clouds of heaven? or hast Thou lighted within me a fire that may burst forth and illumine with force?

Thou knowest that I love Thy word, and that I observe it. Do Thou speak to me of that love which pursues and which searches.

The Master.—Let it be done unto thee as thou desirest; listen thou, and I shall display unto thee new ways, and thou shalt learn the full extent of love as it should exist in the hearts of My disciples.

Truly, truly, do I say unto thee, he who loves dreads neither labour nor pains; he toils, he goes, he comes, he runs, and he never reposes.

He who loves, does he not find in his very love the necessity of revealing itself without ceasing? and this necessity which he feels, is it not as it were an invisible aliment, whose virtue gives him strength?

And the more he acts, the more he desires to act; the more he gives, the more he would still give.

For, does not the mother renew her strength in obeying the voice of her tenderness? And are not the cares she bestows on her new-born babe to her a labour sweeter and more genial than repose?

Learn, then, from those who love according to the flesh, how thou shouldst love according to the spirit.

Many souls have wandered away from God, and in flying from Him they have fled from thy presence, and yet, thou didst await them with love.

Again, many souls have feared to hear thy words, and yet, within the depths of thy heart, thou didst reserve for them a word full of love and of mercy.

O My son, be not discouraged because souls have fled from thy presence, and because they have dreaded the movement of thy lips and the sounds of thy voice.

They have fled, they have feared, as knowing not the love I deposited for them within the depths of thy heart.

Do thou arise in thy force, proceed, and await not their coming, but go thou to them.

It is needful that they should draw near to contemplate thee, and that they should not lose one of those words of life I have confided unto thee, that they may be manifested in their time.

Hasten thou, inasmuch as they flee with the rapidity of the stag pursued by the hunter.

Do thou hasten, and say not that fatigue gains upon thee, and that thou art about to faint, for My charity urges thee.

The eagle discerns his prey from the heights of the clouds, and he displays all the rapidity of his flight in order to rush upon it.

And that which the eagle does for the prey which he would destroy, wherefore shouldst thou not effect for that holy prey which thou shouldst save?

And are not souls as the sacred prey of thy heavenly Father, and hast thou not received the sacred mission of snatching them from the genius of evil?

O, didst thou but know the worth of a soul, thou shouldst no longer delay in opening thy wings, and they should be stronger than those of the eagle.

O, didst thou know the worth of men's souls, thou wouldst reach them more quickly than the ray of light reaches thine eyeballs.

A grain of sand is strong, inasmuch as it arrests in its force the tumultuous waves of the ocean.

And a soul, is it not endowed with greater force than is a grain of sand?

The flower that displays its vivid hues in the green depths of the meadows, and embalms the air with the sweetest of odours, has more of riches in its life than have the pebbles borne down by the torrent that falls from the heights of the mountains.

And is a soul not richer than a flower?

The sun that diffuses his rays on all sides from east to west, and from west to east, and that gives to all living creatures and to all revolving spheres the light which they await, is he not more splendid in his rays than is the flower of the fields in all its hues?

And is not a soul still more splendid than is the sun?

The grain of sand, the flower and the sun are the works of My Father, and these works are great; yet, I say unto thee in truth, all these re-united do not approach in beauty or in force to the least amongst souls.

All these material creatures may be touched by the senses, but the weakest of all human souls is not subject to that slavery.

These creatures are devoid of intelligence, they feel not, neither do they think.

And souls think and feel, and by their thoughts and their sentiments they can elevate themselves to thy heavenly Father, and repose in His divine essence.

The grain of sand, the flower, the sun, act not by their own will, they may not choose between movement and rest, inasmuch as they are not free.

But, souls may act by themselves and choose

between good and evil, between action and inaction, inasmuch as they are free.

And if, being more precious than the grains of sand, than the flowers of the fields, or than the sun that warms thee, why then shouldst thou not draw nigh unto them, wherefore not seek them out in the ardour of thy love?

Thou dost not despise the granite, forasmuch as it may serve thee to some use; and when thou dost build thyself a habitation to shelter thee from the inclemency of the seasons, thou seekest it from afar, and thou dost detach it from the rugged sides of the mountains.

And, thou wouldst not go and seek for those souls which are estranged from My Father?

And knowest thou not, then, that he who seeks one of these souls and who saves it, he builds himself a mansion in heaven?

Thou lovest the flower that raises its head above the verdure of the field, thou drawest nigh to it, thou inhalest its perfume, and thou dost cull it with delight.

And yet, thou wouldst not draw nigh to men's souls, that are more precious in the eyes of My Father than are the lilies of the fields or the roses of the hedges, and those thou wouldst not cull in their misery, to transplant them into the field of the Father.

When the chills of the winter arrive, thou dost flit from place to place in search of some rays of the sun to warm thy members, or, if the heat will not come to warm them, thou leavest thy native land to go, like the wild birds of the air, to dwell in unknown regions, where these rays are more genial.

And yet, thou wouldst not arise to seek in all places that which is more than a ray of the sun, more than the very sun in his splendour.

And dost thou not know that to make these truths comprehensible to the Scribes and the Pharisees, I spoke to them one day in parables, and said to them:

"What man of you, that hath a hundred sheep, and, if he shall lose one of them, doth he not leave the ninety-nine in the desert, and go after that which was lost until he find it?

"And when he hath found it, lay it upon his shoulders rejoicing, and coming home, call together his friends and neighbours, saying to them: Rejoice with me, because I have found my sheep that was lost.

"Now, I say unto thee, that in like manner there shall be more joy in heaven for one sinner who does penance, than for ninety-nine just who have no need of penance."

And, as if that which I had said was not sufficient, turning to these same Pharisees, I said:

"Or what woman having ten groats, if she lose one groat, doth not light a candle, and sweep the house, and seek it diligently until she find it.

"And when she hath found it, call together her friends and neighbours, saying: Rejoice with me, because I have found the groat which I had lost."

"So I say to you, there shall be joy before the angels of God upon one sinner doing penance."

O My son, I have given thee the example that thou mayest walk in My footsteps, I have loved souls with a love that knew no repose.

I, who was seated at the right hand of My Father, I left that right hand that I might come down to this earth, peopled by those living beings who had not as yet passed through the gates of death, which is the passage leading to the true life.

And, when coming into this land of living men, I did not appear in My glory, inasmuch as coming to seek for souls I would not affright them.

And so as not to alarm them, I veiled My glory beneath a soul, like to those I came to seek.

And the souls were not troubled, and they listened to My voice, and they did not fly from Me.

And now, is the disciple greater than his Master? That which the Master has done, why should not the disciple likewise do?

Must thou be evil because I am good, and wilt thou love less, because I love more?

Wherefore standest thou there all day idle, and wherefore dost thou not trouble thyself concerning thy brothers, who stray away from the truth, and who descend from abyss to abyss?

Is not their misery sufficiently great, or, hast thou no love still remaining?

Truly, do I say unto thee, if thy love will not come forth from its repose, it shall perish.

There are souls that come not to thee, go thou

to them; there are others that flee from thee, do thou run to them; and if thou shouldst grow fatigued, run once more. For, does not the heart's fatigue strengthen the heart?

Happy he who understands these things and who practises them, for he guards his soul, and at the end of his course he finds a great joy.

II.

The Disciple.—O, Master! Thou hast said it: he who loves fears not labour; he comes, he goes, and he knows no repose.

Thou willest that I should come forth from my repose, and that I should go to those souls who come not to me; I shall then go, and I shall not be tired of running to them.

Yet, do Thou aid Thy servant in this new way, and let the doctrine of Thy word direct his steps.

O, Master! when I shall draw nigh to a soul that lives remote from Thee, how shall I act?

The shepherd, who leaves the ninety-nine sheep in the desert to run after the one that had gone astray, is sure of bringing back to the fold his lost sheep, inasmuch as he is the stronger.

The woman who searches for her piece of coin, knows that when once found, it shall not escape her, for a piece of money cannot move or elude the grasp of him who takes hold of it.

Lord, so is it not with those who have abandoned Thy ways.

These resist, because the pride of their spirit renders them strong against the truth, and because they will not acknowledge that they were deceived.

They resist, because evil is deeply rooted within them, and because they no longer feel in the depths of their hearts the force to extirpate it.

And when I shall have reached them, how shall I proceed? O, Master! dost Thou not know that I am myself both weak and infirm?

And have I not need of thy force to sustain me along the way, and to preserve wisdom in my heart and justice in my ways?

Can I call forth in its time and display to the children of men the star of the morning, or make the evening star arise above them?

Or can I raise my voice to the clouds, and bid them pour their waters on the earth in abundance?

And, if unable to sustain myself, or to command the stars or the clouds, how may I triumph over those whose eyes will not see Thee, and whose ears will not hear Thee?

The Master.—My son, do not consider thy infirmity or thy weakness, forasmuch as he who loves, abides in God, and he who abides in God is strong.

Is it the husbandman who gives increase to the plants? and yet, if he will cast no grain into the earth, his field shall remain barren.

Be not discouraged, if thou hast not the power

to do the work of God, for thou art but man; do thou the work of man, but perform it well.

Now, behold what shall be thy work, when love shall have guided thee into those gloomy and dismal places where dwell those who separate from Me, that they may in their madness seek life within themselves.

Thou hast walked with rapidity in trying to reach them; but do not so if thou wouldst bring them back.

When the workman would heave up a block of granite, he does not commence like one who but culls a flower.

At first, he examines the angles of the stone, and, without putting his hand to the work, he measures the distance of the angles from the soil.

Thereupon, he introduces the instrument of wood or of iron between the earth and the farthermost angle; he makes an effort, and the stone is upheaved; he makes a second effort, then a third, and the granite stands upright.

Thy task is as that of the workman; behold how he toils, do thou toil in like manner.

As there is not a stone fallen from the summit of the mountain, which does not present an angle by which it may be upraised, so likewise, there is not a man fallen from the pinnacle of virtue, who is not accessible by some corner of his heart.

Thou hast sought afar, and hast found one of thy brothers in whom the pride of the spirit and the breath of the passions have extinguished the life that comes from on high.

Hasten thou, and render this man thy friend, and think not of bringing him the word of life, before his heart has been given to thee.

And, that thou mayest gain his heart, seek not at first to penetrate the secrets of his life, for, he should be guarded against thee, and he would distrust thee.

Speak to him of that which engages thy mind, and fear not to lay open to him a part of thy soul.

They who live the most within themselves, and who are the least confiding of their thoughts, always reveal themselves to those who repose confidence in them.

Therefore, do thou speak of thy joys and thy sorrows, and this thy confidence will quickly force him to confide in thee in his turn.

On his part, he will tell thee that which troubles and wearies him, he will tell thee his successes or reverses, he will speak of his projects, and of those fears and those hopes that lie deep in his heart.

And, if thou wilt listen to him with interest, he shall feel pleasure in being near thee, and his confidences shall become more earnest, and, from the questions of time he shall pass to those questions that interest his soul.

Then, do thou hear him on, and how great soever may be his prejudices or his errors in regard to those truths that surpass by the height of their mystery the conceptions of men, do thou seem neither surprised, or dismayed, or astounded.

A movement, an imprudent word, would seal up his lips, and thou couldst no longer master his spirit, or display the true light to his eyes.

Let him therefore pour out his soul into thine. Let him take all his thoughts, and let him consign them, one by one, to thy breast.

And when a mutual confidence shall have taken place between this man and thee, do thou begin to speak, and thy word shall be welcome.

And that which he could not listen to yesterday, he shall hearken to to-day, and likewise to-morrow.

And he who listens, instructs himself, and he who does not shut his ears to the truth places himself within its action, and his spirit shall ascend from light unto light.

That which he was unable to comprehend yesterday, he shall comprehend to-day, and before the sun will have ended his course, he shall feel his understanding immersed, as it were, in a new life.

And when the true life will have passed into the understanding, it will not cease till it shall have possessed his whole being.

It descends into the vast regions of the heart, and pervading these regions as the blood pervades the whole body, it deposits therein the germ of enduring affections.

And this germ being unfolded by the breath of the Most High, that which was impure in the heart, shall be purified, and that which was not holy, shall become sanctified.

And he whom thou didst seek from afar, shall be

seen standing erect at thy side in the plenitude of force and of honour.

III.

The Disciple.—O, Master! Thou hast revealed unto me the mysteries of the heart; I have seen, and I shall proceed.

I shall do as Thou hast bid me, and he who is in error shall listen to the truth, and he who does evil shall pass into the ways of righteousness.

The Master.—My son, hear Me still on.

The passions arise incessantly within the heart of man, like unto burning winds, and their breath bears far away his holy inspirations.

There is within each man a law of the spirit and a law of the flesh, and the strife between these two laws may frustrate thy work.

The law of the flesh casts into the depths of the understanding thick darkness, and they who are bound beneath this law can hear the truth, yet they understand it not.

And if they comprehend it not, what avails them to have heard it?

The law of the flesh casts into the heart a poisoned germ which destroys all love, and, they who live beneath the empire of this law cannot love the truth.

This law weakens souls, and casts them into languor, and they who follow its dictates lose all courage with all hopes of victory.

And if thus it be, what will it avail them to have loved and comprehended the word of life?

Now, I say unto thee, thou shalt not truly love these souls, if, in displaying to their eyes the true light, thou dost not once more speak to them of the divine gift.

He who comprehends not, does he not need to cherish the hope that he may yet comprehend?

And, he who loves not, does he not need to believe that he can love?

He who regards his infirmity, does he not need to feel nigh to him some visible or invisible force that may reanimate his courage?

And, does not the gift of God dissipate the thickest darkness, does it not open the heart of man to that love which vivifies, and is it not power and force to the weak?

Therefore, do thou reassure him who, having listened to the truth, will not understand it; and reassure him, likewise, who, understanding the truth, does not as yet love it; for if he desires to comprehend and to love it, the divine gift shall come to his aid.

There are two distinct lives for the soul, the one the contemplative, and the other the active; and the divine gift acts incessantly with a view to perfect the soul in each of these lives.

Before thou dost communicate with God by thy

works, thou must first know Him, listen to His mysteries, and learn them.

For, the heavenly gift imparts to thee an exalted idea of divine things, and inspires thee with joy in contemplating them.

It casts rays of light over the understanding that groans in the obscurity of mystery, and those rays, in traversing the soul, dissipate her clouds and bring to her peace, with joy in faith.

It opposes itself to error and ignorance in showing to the soul creatures as they are, and in teaching her how she should judge them.

And, strengthening the mind against doubt, it unveils the arts of the angel of darkness and the deceits of the flesh.

And, when the divine gift has perfected the spirit in the contemplative life, it likewise perfects it in the active.

Egotism, weakness, and pride, are the three great temptations that pursue the heart of man.

And these three temptations precipitate it into terrific responsibilities, those of the neglect of good works, and of the evil into which it succumbs.

And now, My son, do thou reassure him who, after having listened to the truth and comprehended, shall not entertain for it that love which triumphs over all obstacles; for, I say unto thee, if that man desires to love the truth, he shall love it; if he desires to be strong, he shall become strong.

And shall not the gift of God come in aid to his heart, as it has come in aid to his spirit?

And shall it not combat the three temptations that afflict that man?

And shall it not give him a victory over egotism, a victory over weakness, a victory over pride?

He who is alone, nourishes rigour and harshness in the depths of his soul. The miseries of his brothers move him but little, devotedness daunts him, injury awakens guilty instincts within him.

But behold how the divine gift, changing that solitude which is the germ of egotism, breaks all spirit of harshness, inspires love and tenderness, and disperses all the terrors of the soul before real devotedness.

Amongst the children of men there is not one who may rise up and say, "I am strong."

Not one amongst them may undertake an arduous work, without trembling interiorly at the thought of some immediate discouragement.

And when the divine gift shall come, there is not one among those who may not say within the depths of his heart: "What shall I dread? if God be for me, who shall be against me?"

For, does not this gift strengthen the heart of him who is cowardly and weak?

Is not all weakness removed, is not all fear dispelled, so that he who feared to undertake trivial things, now undertakes the greatest of all with a holy courage.

Amongst the children of men, there is not one who does not feel the sting of pride within his mind.

Not one amongst them can undertake the least of all works without self-complacence.

But behold how this gift combats the temptation of pride, through the medium of fear.

Impressing on the mind terrible truths, it humbles within man that which exalts him, and makes him tremble at the sight of the judgments of heaven.

And then, he who took complacence in his works ceases to regard himself, but, fixing his eyes on high, he renders glory to Him from whom proceed all perfect gifts.

And now, that I have shown thee where thou mayest find love, with strength and intelligence, go thou, and bring joy to thy brother who mourns.

He has need to hope that he shall comprehend the truth, and do thou display unto him the gift of God, which is a gift of intelligence.

He has need to hope that his heart will love that which his mind will comprehend, and that a secret and invisible force will aid him to walk in the ways of justice; and do thou display unto him the divine gift, which is a gift of strength and of love.

When a man feels himself alone in presence of a work surpassing his strength, he grows dismayed, and will undertake nothing.

But, does another come to his aid, he arises directly; and, forgetting his weakness, he commences his task.

And, so is it with the souls that live far from My Father.

When these souls, within which the spirit of truth has as yet been unable to produce a clear light, when these souls consider themselves, they find themselves isolated, and their solitude causes them to fall into languor.

But, let them see the divine gift coming to them; let them know it, and, glorying in their infirmity, they will receive the task with love, and they shall exult with joy in the holocaust.

IV.

The Master.—The greatest teaching does not consist in words, but example; and, to the end that this teaching may not be wanting to thee, do thou hear Me still on.

I shall manifest to thee Mine own actions, and thine eyes shall see how the Son of Man came forth from the place of His repose to seek that which was lost, and to revive that which was dead.

Desiring to leave Judea and repair to Galilee, I traversed the land of Samaria, and arrived at a small town named Sichar.

In that town was the fountain of Jacob; fatigued by My course, I seated Myself on the brink of that fountain. It was about the sixth hour.

There cometh a woman of Samaria to draw water, and I said to her: Give Me to drink. For My disciples were gone into the city to buy meats.

Then that Samaritan woman saith to Me: "How dost Thou, being a Jew, ask of me to drink, who am a Samaritan woman, for the Jews do not communicate with the Samaritans."

I answered, and said to her: "If thou didst know the gift of God, and who He is that saith to thee: Give Me to drink, thou perhaps wouldst have asked of Him, and He would have given thee living water."

The woman saith to Me: "Sir, Thou hast nothing wherein to draw, and the well is deep; from whence then hast Thou living water?

"Art Thou greater than our father Jacob, who gave us the well, and drank thereof himself, and his children, and his cattle?"

I answered, and said to her: "Whosoever drinketh of this water shall thirst again, but he that shall drink of the water that I shall give him, shall not thirst for ever.

"But, this water that I shall give him shall become in him a fountain of water springing up into life everlasting."

The woman saith to Me: "Sir, give me this water, that I may not thirst, nor come hither to draw."

I said to her, "Go, call thy husband, and come hither;" the woman answered and said: "I have no husband."

I said to her, "Thou hast said well, I have no husband, for thou hast had five husbands; and he whom thou now hast is not thy husband: this thou hast said truly."

The woman saith to Me: "Sir, I perceive Thou art a prophet. Our fathers adored on this mountain; and You say that at Jerusalem is the place where men must adore."

I said to her, "Woman, believe Me, the hour cometh, when you shall neither on this mountain nor in Jerusalem adore the Father.

"You adore that which you know not, we adore that which we know, for salvation is of the Jews.

"But, the hour cometh, and now is, when the true adorers shall adore the Father in spirit and in truth. For the Father also seeketh such to adore Him.

"God is a spirit, and they that adore Him, must adore Him in spirit and in truth."

The woman saith to Me: "I know that the Messias cometh, who is called Christ, therefore, when He is come, He will tell us all things."

I said to her, "I am He who am speaking with thee." And immediately My disciples came, and they wondered that I talked with the woman.

Yet, no man said, What seekest Thou, or why talkest Thou with her?

The woman, therefore, left her water-pot, and went her way into the city, and saith to the men there: "Come and see a Man who hath told me all things whatsoever I have done.

"Is He not the Christ?" They went therefore out of the city, and came unto Me.

O My son! I have told thee, he who loves souls

comes, and goes, without ever reposing. And now, am I not He who loves souls?

I leave Judea, and pass through Samaria in returning to Galilee, is it not love that guides My steps?

I know that a woman shall come at the sixth hour of the day to the brink of the fountain of Jacob to fetch water, and I go to repose Myself on the brink of that fountain; is it not the labour of love that I seek before rest?

That woman comes, I do not terrify her, I do not say to her: The kingdom of God is nigh, let him hear who has ears, and let him understand who can understand.

In coming to cure her soul, I seek to gain her heart; and as the heart inclines towards those whom it solaces, I say to that woman of Samaria, Woman, give Me to drink.

She replies to Me: "How happens it that Thou, who art a Jew, askest to drink of a woman of Samaria, whereas the Jews have no communication with the Samaritans?"

Behold, that woman stands amazed, yet, in that amazement there is joy, inasmuch as heart does not resist heart.

And, availing Myself of the joy I had awaked within her, I reply to her; she comprehends not My meaning, but I reassure her in showing unto her the divine gift: O didst thou but know the gift of God!

Consoled by this word, she listens to Me, all

enmity has disappeared from her soul, and for her there is now neither Jew nor Samaritan.

She listens to Me, I speak of a wonderful water, saying unto her: Whosoever drinks of the water which I shall give him shall never thirst; and it shall become in him a fountain of water springing up to life everlasting.

Now, even as I confided in her in asking of her the water which she comes to draw at the fountain of Jacob, so in like manner does she confide in Me, saying: "Lord, give me of the water of which Thou dost speak, that I may never thirst."

And, seeing that that woman confides in Me, I then lay open to her the depths of her heart, and show her all its miseries.

The hour is nigh when the divine gift is to descend into her soul, for behold how, no longer resisting the truth of My word, she exclaims: "Lord, Thou art a prophet."

And then, urged by the necessity of knowing the truth, she asks Me many other questions, and as I say to her those words: "I am the Messias, I who speak to thee," the light is made within her.

Thou seest that woman, she is far away from Me, I go to seek her; her mind is immersed in darkness, I speak with her a language that she does not comprehend, I wait till friendship shall be formed within her heart, to reveal to her the most intimate secrets; and that revelation opens her eyes.

She perceives not as yet the whole truth, but

she desires to see it, and that vision is given her.

Do thou go, as does the Son of Man, towards him who comes not to thee.

Speak, and if thy language be not understood, be not disquieted.

Make known the gift of God, and, when a mutual confidence shall be established betwixt thee and thy brother, do thou then discover to him the miseries of his heart.

That revelation shall open his eyes, he shall desire to comprehend, and God shall come to his aid.

SEVENTH COLLOQUY.

THE DISCIPLE HAS SPOKEN WITH THE SOULS, AND THEY HAVE HEARKENED TO HIS VOICE; YET, NOTWITHSTANDING, BEHOLD SORROW RE-ENTERS HIS HEART.—HE HAS BEHELD THESE SOULS TAKE A HOLY FLIGHT TOWARDS THE PURE AND CELESTIAL SPHERES, AND NOW HE HAS CEASED TO SEE THEM.—HE DEMANDS OF THE MASTER IF THERE BE IN THE FIRE OF LOVE SOME GERM, POTENT AND FERTILE, THAT MAY RAISE THAT WHICH WAS FALLEN AND REVIVE THAT WHICH IS DEAD.—THE MASTER REPLIES, HE WHO LOVES, PARDONS, AND PARDON UPRAISES SOULS; HE RECOMMENDS HIS DISCIPLE TO PARDON SEVENTY TIMES SEVEN TIMES.

THE MASTER TEACHES ALL THESE THINGS BY HIS EXAMPLE.

SEVENTH COLLOQUY.

I.

The Disciple.—O Master! I have entered into Thy ways, because my heart has comprehended Thy word.

I have not reposed in my solitude, I have run, because Thou didst excite within me a thirst that consumed me, and that thirst was that of souls.

And, when I found those who wandered astray, and who erred in the counsels of their mind, I spoke to them as Thou didst tell me.

I reached the door of their hearts, I knocked, and their hearts were opened, they came to me, whereas I had gone to them.

I pressed their hand, they pressed my hand in return; I gave them the kiss of peace, and they responded to me.

And, perceiving they were not daunted in my presence, seeing that friendship had dawned within them, I brought them Thy word, which is the word of life.

They heard that word, and it seemed as though sadness entered their souls, because they understood it not, because they loved it not, because they felt not within them the strength to reduce it to practice.

And I dispelled all sadness within them, because I showed unto them the gift of God, by which men are enabled to comprehend, and to love, and to practice the things which are above the reach of the understanding and heart.

And now, as knowing the divine gift, they asked for it, and this gift came to their aid, and it rendered possible those things that seemed impossible, and their steps were assured in the ways of wisdom.

I have seen souls rise from their infirmities, as I see the plants that grow in the depths of the waters appear after a time above the abyss that covered their heads.

I have seen them take a holy flight towards the pure and heavenly regions; their course was more rapid than is that of the stars that move in the infinite regions of space; and now, I see them no longer.

I seek them on the surface of the deep, and I find them not; I seek them on the way that leads to our heavenly home, and I meet them not.

After having seen, they have closed their eyes, that they might cease to see; they have driven away love, as though love had wearied their hearts.

And now, how may I hope to establish harmony amongst souls? My work, is it not as the flower of the fields, that unfolds in the morning, to wither away by the evening?

O Master! how shall I act? is there within the fire of charity some germ, fertile and potent, which may raise that which is fallen, and revive that which is dead?

And, if such germ exists, O grant that mine eye may behold it, do Thou deign to unfold it within me, that I may be strong by its power, as I am strong by Thy word.

The Master.—My son, disquiet not thyself, he who loves, pardons, and pardon bears up the souls that were fallen.

Be thou merciful, as thy heavenly Father is merciful; and so thou wilt save thy brother who has erred.

Love seeks not to lose, but to save; it seeks not to estrange, but it attracts; it irritates not the wound, but it probes it.

And does not thy heavenly Father cause His sun to rise on the good and the evil? Does He not give to the evil the earth which sustains them, the air that they breathe, the garments that cover them, the bread that sustains them?

He loves the just, and He abandons not the wicked, for, He wills not the death of the impious; He wills that he should abandon his errors and live.

He will not repulse the men of iniquity, but He attracts them by His word and His promise, and His word is sweet and affectionate as that of the mother in soothing her babe, and His promises are divine and infallible.

He calls these men "My people," when they will no longer be His people.

Like unto a man who fears he has offended his friend, He draws nigh, and says unto him: "What have I done unto thee, and how have I displeased thee? Answer me."

The men of iniquity reply not, ingratitude has penetrated their hearts, yet My Father who is in heaven is not wearied.

He attracts them by the promise of His mercy. "Children of men," He says, "your iniquities are more numerous than the hairs of your heads, or than the sands of the sea, but, fear ye not, for I am twice merciful before I am just.

"If My justice were impatient, and if it strengthened My arm against you, should not your earth be parched up by My wrath, as the grass is parched up by a scorching ray of the sun.

"But, whereas My mercy triumphs over My justice, behold how I shall pardon all your crimes, behold how I shall cause My grace to abound where sin hath abounded.

"I am nigh unto you, in order to re-establish all things, not alone in entirety, but even in abundance.

"Let your hearts be not disquieted, believe in Me, and confide in My mercy, await Me, and I shall come, and I shall heal you.

"Be converted to Me, and I shall be converted unto you. Let your prayer ascend towards My throne as the smoke of the incense, and I shall hear it. Abandon your ways, and I shall forget all your errors.

"You have outraged and contemned Me, who have nourished and fostered you; you have trampled Me under foot, as the wayfarer treads on the insect that crosses his path.

"And, I ask but one tear from you, and with that tear I shall blot out your name from the book of death."

It is after this manner, O My son, that thy heavenly Father is merciful.

And now, wherefore should thy heart be as though it were weighed down by harshness, wherefore should it not reveal by its mercy the mercy of thy Father who is in heaven?

Who art thou, who wilt not use mercy?

Art thou not man? and man born of woman, does he not live but a short space, and is his life not filled with miseries?

The course of his days is arrested; as the tent of the shepherd is rolled up, even so is he removed and is snatched away.

The Almighty cuts the thread of his life, as the weaver severs the piece in his loom, and whilst his web is still lengthening out, the hand of the Most High rends it asunder.

This morning sees his birth, and by evening time, he is about to die.

Who art thou, who wilt not use mercy?

Hast thou not been conceived in iniquity, and art thou not born a child of wrath?

Do thou sound thy heart, is it sufficiently

pure to deny its indulgence and its compassion to those who wander astray?

Those men whom thou dost repulse with harshness, may they not exclaim: "Thou hypocrite, who art severe, where are thine own virtues?

"The thoughts of our minds, the desires of our hearts, the acts of our will, are they not thy thoughts, and thy desires, and thy actions?

"Hypocrite! thou wouldst impose on us a burden that thou wouldst not touch with the tip of thy finger."

My son, thy heart is not like to that of the wicked, thy word does not rise up against God, thou dost not partake of their licentiousness and their pleasures; but, art thou for that reason exempt from sin? Do not the very just fall seven times?

Thou despisest those amongst thy brothers who do not mortify their senses, and who abandon themselves to gross pleasures, and thou dost not reflect that pride consumes thy heart, even as the vulture devours his prey.

The least contradiction irritates thee; thou dost ambition the influence exercised by others; thy spirit is disquieted, because it does not direct and govern all according to its caprices.

Dost thou not speak over-much of thyself, of the works of beneficence thou undertakest, of the sciences thou hast acquired, of the success thou obtainest?

Thy pride insinuates itself everywhere, even into thy purest and holiest conversations.

In speaking of thy spiritual misery, dost thou not seek to appear humble in the eyes of men?

When thou givest counsel, dost thou not feel a secret complacency in assuming the tone of a master and of a zealous reformer?

At each instant of thy life, thou hast need that the mercy of the celestial Father should be exercised above thee; and yet, thou wouldst not be merciful in favour of others.

Didst thou know thyself, thou shouldst be more indulgent in regard to thy brothers.

This knowledge would reveal to thee the weakness and the frailty of men, and thy heart would unfold to a sweet commiseration for them.

Thou art severe, because thou dost believe thyself perfect, and thy severity shall convince thee of error, on the day of judgment.

II.

The Master.—Thou hast seen all the breadth and the depth of the mercy of thy heavenly Father, behold once more how great is the mercy of the Son of Man.

As the hour was late, I repaired one day to the Mountain of Olives; after having there passed the night, as I was wont, at break of day I returned to the temple, whither all the people came to Me.

And, as I instructed the people, the Scribes and

Pharisees led to Me a woman taken in adultery, and set her in the midst of the assembly.

They said to Me: "Master, this woman was even now taken in adultery. Now, Moses in the law commanded to stone such a one, but what sayest Thou?"

And this they said tempting Me, that they might accuse Me.

But, bowing Myself down, I wrote with My finger on the ground.

They understood not My silence, and desirous to find in My reply matter for their calumnies, they persisted in questioning Me.

With that, rising up, I said to them: "Let him amongst you who is free from sin cast the first stone."

And again, stooping down, I wrote on the ground.

But they, hearing this, went out one by one, beginning at the eldest, and I alone remained, and the woman standing in the midst.

Then, lifting Myself up, I said to her: "Woman, where are they that accused thee? Hath no man condemned thee?" Who said: "No man, Lord."

And I said: "Neither will I condemn thee. Go and sin no more."

O My son! be careful in believing that in displaying this great mercy, I only sought to humble the pride of the Scribes and Pharisees.

Or else, that in saving this woman from the fearful punishment that was reserved for her according to the law, I only sought to save her mortal existence.

I say unto thee, in truth, that that which I willed, that which I sought above all other things, was the salvation of her soul.

I loved that soul, and in My love I felt that I should not abandon it to a confusion that would have arrested within her heart all impulse towards good.

And, in order to dispel the extreme confusion that covered her face, I turned to her accusers, saying to them: "Let him who is free from sin cast the first stone."

They heard, and the confusion passed from the soul of the sinner into their hearts, they entered into themselves and retired.

Their flight had prepared a work of salvation.

She who had scarcely breathed beneath the weight of her condemnation, already breathed more freely; delivered from her enemies, joy was revived in her soul, yet, that joy was not complete.

It was still needful to perfect the work of salvation, and, searching amidst the treasures of My love, I found a word of life in the words of pardon.

And how might I have saved her soul, had I not pardoned her?

The word of pardon, is it not a word of life which reanimates that which was dead through sin, in restoring the courage of the heart?

And, is there not a bond of love established between him who pardons and him who is pardoned? and this invisible bond, is it not a resurrection?

Behold that woman! surprised in her crime, she is dragged by the hands of men to the place of her punishment.

The sight of the tortures that await her troubles her soul; her heart beats, but it is not love which causes it to beat, it is fear.

Her heart throbs, and in its throbbings, it may be, there is hatred against those who would put her to death.

The harshness of men has aggravated her misery, as the two-edged sword enlarges the wound in which it is violently stirred.

She was guilty but of one fault; but, troubled within herself, she feels other remorses arise within her soul.

Let her eyes see mercy shine forth, let her feel the divine touch of pardon; and then, her heart shall cease to be agonized by fear or tortured by hatred.

It shall unfold to that tenderness that is productive of tears, and, these tears shall be the tears of repentance.

O My son, there is a confusion that proceeds from God, and that is fruitful in good; and there is yet another confusion proceeding from men, and that is productive of evil.

Therefore, suffer not this latter to take hold of him who has erred.

But, leave in his heart that confusion that comes from God, for, this casts into the soul a germ of sorrow, which does not stifle within her the germs of confidence.

Thou must not be wanting to the soul that has become estranged from My Father; and, if thy presence reveal not to her that she may still hope, wilt thou not be wanting to her?

When thou shalt have dispelled that extreme confusion which produces evil, wilt thou not have commenced a work of salvation?

In order to return to righteousness, is it not needful to experience an internal liberty; and an extreme confusion, is it not slavery?

And that slavery, does it not plunge the soul into the depths of obscurity, does it not efface the sentiment of her actuality, as likewise the sentiment of that which she might become by virtue of that force which comes from on high?

Truly, truly, do I say unto thee, it happens to many that, owing to the confusion coming from men, their state is rendered still worse than at first.

They would have arisen from their misery, whereas they have remained in their evil ways; they would have broken their chains, and they have riveted them on their hearts.

Therefore, do thou hasten to deliver the soul that thou shalt find crushed beneath the weight of that shame and that sorrow that are productive of evil.

It is then thou wilt have commenced a great work of salvation, and, in order to consummate it, thou shalt search as the Son of Man sought in

His love, and, therein thou shalt likewise find a word of life in the words of pardon.

Till now, thou hast not done this good work, because thou didst not sufficiently detach thy heart from thyself in the work thou didst undertake, for the sake of thy brothers.

Thou didst bestow looks of complaisance on the success of thy words and thy counsels, and behold, why thou couldst not endure their fall without being interiorly discouraged and troubled.

And whereas trouble and discouragement are the seeds of bad passions, pride has entered thy spirit, and harshness has taken hold of thy heart.

Thou hast repulsed, and not attracted, thou hast enlarged the wounds, instead of closing them.

Truly, do I say unto thee, he who loves, seeks not himself in his love; he loves in God, and thus loving, trouble and discouragement never will crush him.

He supports contradiction with patience, he is not surprised at evil, and his heart retains that force that produces tears in life, and life in tears.

III.

The Disciple.—Till now I had only heard the word of man, and that word is harder than the iron, colder than the marble.

O my Master! hadst Thou not spoken to me, my mind would never have elevated itself to a doctrine thus sublime, and my heart should have remained, as it were, buried under a weight of eternal frost.

But, behold how I commence this day to comprehend that which I had never before comprehended; behold how my soul grows transformed, behold how the knowledge of her weakness brings with it already the feeling of a mercy still greater.

O Master! I sigh after Thy words, as the thirsty stag sighs after the fountains of living water; do Thou speak, speak continually, and do Thou quench this thirst of mine.

The Master.—The spirit is willing, but the flesh is weak, therefore, do I say unto thee, he who loves pardons seventy times seven times.

Are not the children of men the sons of the same father, and that father, was he not guilty from the commencement?

Behold the first man! God had formed him upright. He had fixed within him His dwelling, in establishing within him the seat of His justice!

That man He had gifted with liberty, full and entire, and with that liberty a will upright and inclined to all good.

He had endowed him with discernment, He had gifted him with the light of intelligence.

He had created within him the knowledge of the spirit, He had filled his heart with sentiment, He had shown him the good and the evil.

He had darted the beams of His eye into his heart, that he might see the greatness of His work, that he might exalt by his homage the sanctity of His name, that he might extol Him for His wonders, that he might publish the magnificence of His works.

And now, hast thou not seen him who was created in holiness and in justice, hast thou not seen him suffer himself to be seduced in his force?

Hast thou not seen him become like unto the reed, which is shaken by the slightest breeze?

Hast thou not seen the light of his spirit vanish in a cloud of thick darkness, and the affections of his heart grow troubled, and his flesh rebel when moved by the breath of impure fancies?

And dost thou not know that that man transmitted to all of his race the darkness of his spirit, and with its darkness, the insubordination of his heart, with the appetites of his flesh?

Wherefore, then, should an excess of discouragement lay hold on thee, if thy brother should fall many times on his way?

Thy brother, and all thy brethren, and thou

thyself, are you not the children of that first man?

And if he who had been created in strength and in justice, if he became weak in the hour of temptation, they who are conceived in iniquity, shall they not be still weaker?

Behold these last, they feel in the members of their bodies another law that combats against the law of their spirit, and which renders them captive under the law of sin which abides in their members.

And wilt thou not pardon those till seventy times seven times?

Thick darkness envelops them from the commencement, and this they cannot, without great efforts, dispel.

And wilt thou not pardon them till seventy times seven times?

Their spirit is agitated by doubts and perplexities that return at each hour of the day.

And these doubts, these anxieties of the soul, expose them unceasingly to the fascinations of error and falsehood.

And canst thou not pardon them till seventy times seven times?

Disorderly passions tempt them to turn away from the ways of justice, and give birth in their hearts to evil desires, and in their insatiable thirst, they are forcibly driven to drink of the muddy waters.

And canst thou not pardon them seventy times seven times?

They combat their evil appetites, and they ask themselves at the close of the day: "Have we fought valiantly?"

They implore aid from on high, they pray their heavenly Father for wisdom, and for love, and for strength; and they ask of themselves at the close of the day: "Have we prayed aright?"

They suffer with patience, they offer their tribulations to Him who changes all pains into an immense weight of glory; and at evening time they ask of themselves: "Have we suffered as we ought?"

They have fought bravely, they have prayed well, they have suffered well; but, as not knowing this, their heart is steeped in sadness, and this sadness has discouraged them in the combat.

And, canst thou not pardon them till seventy times seven times?

My son, do thou not say that he who falls frequently is unworthy of pardon; for, truly I say unto thee, every man whose heart begins to hate evil, and to aspire after good, is deserving of pardon.

Say not thou, that all they who detest evil to-day, and who succumb to-morrow, have not within them a true sorrow; forasmuch as grace and concupiscence confront each other, as enemy stands opposed to enemy.

When grace descends into the hearts of the children of men, their spirit is prompt, they see the good, and they love it; and, loving it, they are impelled by a holy impulse to advance in the ways of righteousness.

When concupiscence arises within them, the flesh is feeble, as before an impetuous wind that comes to overthrow all on its way, and throws nature into disorder.

It is then that they lose the clear vision of all things just and good; and, the allurements of evil being reawakened by the exterior senses, the soul falls, as it were, into oblivion of all that which it had previously loved.

They fall, but, when fallen, their lips contract as those of a man who has eaten of a bitter fruit.

Now, I say unto thee, this bitterness is, as it were, the commencement of that grace which shall revive them once more.

There are some who dread to pardon continually him who makes frequent falls, and, these men do much evil, inasmuch as if one do not hasten to raise by forgiveness him who is fallen, shall not the love of wisdom languish within him, and shall he not shortly commence to drink iniquity like water?

If these men knew themselves better, as likewise their fallen brothers, and their brothers who may still fall, they would incessantly open their hearts, in order to succour each living soul in her misery.

They would be merciful, as the heavenly Father is merciful, and the excess of their charity would produce abundant fruits of salvation.

My son, dost thou remember this word of Mine, "the spirit is willing, but the flesh is weak"? Do thou judge thy brothers by this word, forasmuch as he who will thus judge, will not condemn them.

He shall see how great is the weakness of men, he shall behold the struggles that arise in their hearts at each moment, and he shall measure the force of the passions.

He shall see the difficulty of separating the pure from the impure, in the passions of man.

He shall behold that fatal power exercised by the exterior senses over all that is most holy in the affections of the soul, and he shall see how much that power weakens and deadens her freedom.

And, beholding these things, he shall understand that the salvation of his brothers is in this word of life:

You shall pardon till seventy times seven times.

IV.

The Disciple.—O Master! I have seen men whom the world regards as just, their morals are austere, on their face there beams a something celestial, yet these men do not practice the words Thou hast spoken to me.

What shall I then do if I deviate from the ways

which they follow, shall I not be regarded as a man deceiving himself?

Will they not style my charity a crime, and will they not seek to repulse me, as a dangerous man, who strews a subtle venom over his path?

The Master.—There are no just men, save those who walk in My footsteps, and who seek to imitate My example.

Be not disquieted by reason of him who believes he acts rightly in interpreting all My words according to his spirit; for, I say unto thee, that man is blinded by his own doctrine.

I have oftentimes pardoned, and in thus pardoning I have performed great things amongst men.

I have created a pure heart, and I have re-established an upright spirit within them.

I have rendered unto them the joy of My assistance, and I have confirmed them in giving them a spirit of force.

Was it not in frequently pardoning that I confirmed in truth and in justice that apostle to whom I confided the keys of the kingdom of heaven?

Before I had strengthened him by many words of pardon, was not he that apostle Peter, weak and pusillanimous?

One evening, in walking upon the waters, I come up to the bark of My disciples, and reach them towards the fourth watch of the night.

They distinguish Me through the darkness, and not recognizing Me, they become terrified; with one word I reassure them, and Peter, who hears

My voice, exclaims: "Lord, if it be Thou, bid me come to Thee upon the waters."

And I said: "Come;" and Peter, going down out of the boat, walked upon the water to come to Me.

And, seeing the wind strong, he was afraid; and when he began to sink, he cried out, saying: "Lord, save me."

And immediately, stretching forth My hand, I took hold of him, and said to him: "O thou of little faith, why dost thou doubt?"

Behold that man, he knows that if I will it so he shall walk on the waters as on the granite of the mountains; he comes forth, he comes to Me, and the waves grow firm under his feet.

A higher wind arises, and he fears, as if unknowing that He who can give solidity and consistency to the waves, can likewise by one word lay the winds and the tempests.

He fears, his soul is troubled, and it is at this same instant that I operate a prodigy in his favour.

And now, how did I act? Did I leave him to perish who had offended Me in doubting of My power, at the moment when he experienced its effects?

No; I extended My hand, I sustained his trembling members over the deep, I raised him in pardoning him.

Yet, another evening I went with My disciples beyond the torrent of Cedron, and I arrived at a place called Gethsemani.

And, having reached that place, I said unto My disciples: "Sit you here till I go yonder and pray; watch ye, and pray that ye enter not into temptation."

With that, leaving the others, I took with Me Peter, James, and John, and I began to fear and to be filled with sadness.

And I said to them: "My soul is sorrowful even unto death; stay you here and watch with Me."

And, advancing, I removed from them the distance of a stone's throw, and, kneeling, I prayed in these words:

Father, let this chalice pass away from Me. Nevertheless, not as I will, but as Thou wilt. And, falling, as it were, into an agony, I continued to pray still more earnestly. "My Father," I said, "all things are possible to Thee; if this chalice may not pass away, but I must drink it, Thy will be done;" and My body was bathed in a sweat of blood that fell down in drops to the earth.

Then, there appeared to Me an angel of light, who came to comfort Me.

And, rising up after My prayer, I went to My disciples, and I found them sleeping from sadness.

I said to Peter: "Simon, sleepest thou? Couldst thou not watch one hour with Me? Watch and pray, that you may not enter into temptation. The spirit is willing, but the flesh is weak."

Retiring for the second time, I offered the same

prayer: "Father, if it be possible, let this chalice pass from Me; nevertheless, not as I will, but as Thou wilt;" and, returning to them, I found them sleeping, and they knew not what to answer Me.

And, leaving them, I retired once more, and the third time I made the same prayer.

I then returned to My disciples, and I said to them: "Sleep ye now and take your rest; but behold the hour is come when the Son of Man shall be betrayed into the hands of sinners. Rise up, let us go; behold, he who will betray Me is at hand."

Behold that apostle to whom I had already pardoned his fear and his want of faith when walking on the waters.

I warned him that the spirit is willing, but that the flesh is weak, and that it is expedient to watch and pray, so as not to enter into temptation.

I say to him that My soul is sorrowful even unto death, and I ask of him a first time to pray with Me.

I leave him for an instant, together with James and John, and, he does not obey My orders, but falls asleep.

I go to him, and the second time repeat the same request, but he does not obey Me, and sleeps again.

I retire once more, and when I return I find his eye heavy, and he knows not what to answer Me.

And now, what did I do? Did I repulse that man, so cowardly, and so faithless to My word?

Did I say unto him: "Simon, Simon, thou couldst not watch one hour with Me; return to thy bark and to thy nets, retire far from that Master whom thou knowest not how to serve in His sorrow, or sustain in His anguish"?

No, I do not repulse him, I pardon him his cowardice, in calling him once more to Me. "Arise," I say to him, "let us go; behold he comes who is to deliver Me up." Thereupon Peter arose.

And now, believe not thou that this prevarication of his was the last, and that this pardon was the last accorded by the Son of Man.

That same night on which I was steeped in a sweat of blood that flowed down to the earth, I was arrested by a troop of armed men.

And these men, seizing on Me, led Me to the house of the High Priest, and Peter followed Me from a distance.

And reaching the house of Caiphas, his people having lighted a fire in the midst of the courtyard, Peter likewise seated himself amongst them.

And there came to him a servant maid, saying: "Thou also wast with Jesus the Galilean." But he denied before them all, saying: "I know not what thou sayest."

As he went out of the gate, another maid saw him, and saith to them that were there: "This man also was with Jesus of Nazareth."

And again he denied with an oath: "That I know not the man."

And, after a little while, they came that stood

by, and said to Peter: "Surely, thou art one of them, for even thy speech doth discover thee."

Then he began to curse and swear, that he knew not the man; and immediately the cock crew. And Peter remembered the words which I had said: "Before the cock crows, thou shalt deny Me thrice;" and, going out, he wept bitterly.

Behold, once more, this apostle to whom I had just pardoned his guilty slumber.

He follows Me into the house of the High Priest, but, weak and pusillanimous, he follows Me at a distance.

He seats himself in the midst of My enemies, but it is not in order to defend Me.

They question him concerning Me, and he answers with an oath, that he knows Me not, and that he has never been of the number of My disciples.

And now, what shall I do? He has been ashamed of Me, and shall I not likewise renounce him?

He has refused to bestow on Me one look that might proclaim that he followed Me, as being his Master.

Shall I, on My part, refuse to cast a look on him, a look of pardon, to reveal to him that although he abandoned Me, I shall not renounce him, and that although he denied Me, yet I will not deny him for My disciple.

No, I bestow on him this look of love, and Peter comprehends it; he sees that I pardon him his fault, and seeing that, he goes out and weeps bitterly.

O My son, had I not used this great mercy, should I have confirmed in faith and in justice him who should one day confirm his brethren?

For, should not harshness have shattered that rock on which I would found My Church, which I sanctified by My blood?

Had I not said to My Father, that of all those He had given Me I should not lose one? and how should I not have lost him who denied Me, had I withheld from him that look in which he was to read My love and My pardon?

Even as did the Son of Man, so do thou not lose one of those whom the Father has given thee; and when the relapses of thy brother shall come to rend thy soul, forget not this word of Mine:

"The spirit is willing, but the flesh is weak."

V.

The Disciple.—O Master! nothing is hidden from Thine eyes, of all that which passes in the hearts of men, and, behold why the word of pardon has never fallen from Thy lips without being a gift of life.

Thou didst pardon seventy times seven times, but Thou didst sound the hearts and the loins, and thus sounding them, Thou didst read grief and repentance.

As to me, in what manner may I follow Thy instructions? Is not my glance that of man, and that glance, can it penetrate into souls?

How may I use Thy spirit of mercy without abusing that spirit, and if I should abuse it, shall not my fallen brethren be more guilty in Thine eyes than they were at first?

The Master.—My son, he who loves, pardons always, because he always prepares the ways of pardon; and that is why I say unto thee: "Do thou prepare these ways, and fear not."

When thou shalt encounter souls parched up by the heat of evil, as plants separated from their stems are scorched by the rays of the burning sun, do thou not leave these souls till thou hast called down to them that sorrow that renders them worthy of an immense mercy.

There are some who do evil, forasmuch as, distracted by the works of this earth, their understanding has not soared to the splendours of truth, and for these do thou prepare the ways of pardon, in teaching them things to which they were strangers.

There are some, again, who commit evil, because the passions of the heart have been set in contradiction to the lights of the understanding, for those prepare the ways of pardon, in showing them that there is no true joy, save in the peace which comes from the Almighty.

Others, again, there are who do evil, because they say within themselves: "The measure is complete; we have received much, and we have abused all that which we received, and it is too late still to hope."

Do thou prepare for these last the ways of pardon, in teaching them that the heavenly Father is not a harsh and severe Master, who demands back of His servants all that which He has given them.

They have received much, and they have left to perish in their hands the most precious of gifts, yet, that which they cannot give back shall not be demanded of them.

Yet, let sorrow but penetrate them, and let confidence accompany that sorrow, and the Almighty shall no longer remember their abuse of His graces, or the talents they have buried.

Thou canst not, as did the Son of Man, impart a heavenly virtue that can change in the course of an instant the hardest of hearts.

Make Him known, from whom proceeds that heavenly virtue. Thou canst not by a word or a look communicate to hearts the holy and ineffable sadness of repentance, and that, because thy look is not divine, and because thy word is but human.

Do thou make Him known whose look is divine, and whose word is all-powerful.

Did men only know Me, they should know that I trampled underfoot all pride of the spirit in assuming the form of the slave, and they should detest those emotions of pride that render them guilty in the eyes of the Father, whereas they are not in conformity with the image of His Son.

They would know that although the foxes have

their dens, and whilst the birds of the air have their nests, yet, with a view to humble all covetousness and love of things of the earth, I had not a stone to pillow My head, and they would conceive an aversion to that love and that covetousness.

They would know that, with the intent to purify all flesh from the contamination of sense, I suffered My head to be crowned with thorns and My body to be torn by the blows of the scourge.

They would know that the Sacred Humanity of the Son of Man was abandoned to the outrages of His judges and to the brutality of their soldiers.

And, knowing all these things, they would recall all their iniquities in the bitterness of their souls, and the tears they would shed should be those of love and of confidence.

O My son, do thou study thy Master in His words and His actions, and when thou wilt have thus studied Him, thou wilt reveal the tenderness of His heart, and this revelation shall touch the worst and the most hardened of men.

Then shall they enter into those ways that shall render them worthy of the grace of His pardon, because, after having sinned much, they shall hear a secret voice saying unto them:

"'You may hope much."

VI.

The Disciple.—O Master! that same night on which an angel came to strengthen Thee, I followed Thy steps along the paths of Gethsemani, and I perceived one of Thine own deliver Thee into the hands of sinners.

I saw the perfidious disciple come at the head of an armed band, and betray Thee with a kiss.

At that same hour, I heard a sweet voice coming from Thy heart, bespeaking more of love and of sadness than could a tear falling from the eyelids.

For, Thou didst say to the traitor: "My friend, wherefore art thou come here?"

And he, the traitor, on hearing that word, answered not, he carried back the thirty pieces of silver to the princes of the priests and the ancients, and went and hung himself in despair.

And yet he knew Thee, he had seen the wonders of Thy right hand, he had assisted at that last repast wherein Thou didst make the most sublime of testaments.

He knew Thou wast the Christ, the Son of the living God, and that Thou hadst never refused to remit the sins of the children of men.

Although thus knowing Thee, he perceived not that there was to be found in Thee a remedy for all imaginable distress, yet no holy tears flowed from his eyes.

O, my Master! if thus it be with those who know Thee, how may I still hope to prepare within the souls of men the ways of pardon, in revealing to them Thy divine charity?

The Master.—Believe not thou that he who betrayed the Son of Man in the paths of Gethsemani in reality knew the Son of Man.

He had eyes, and he would not see, he had ears, and he would not hear.

If he had known Me, he should have comprehended My heart, in seeing that I repelled not his kiss.

He had seen the disciple John reposing on My breast, but he knew that My lips did not approach those of that disciple whom I loved amongst all others.

And, had he known Me, should he not have understood that in accepting his kiss I made a supreme effort in order to break the obduracy of his soul?

He knew that I had extended My hand to the disciple Peter, when he was sinking on the waters, saying to him: "Man of little faith, wherefore hast thou doubted?"

And, had he known Me, should he not have comprehended the sweetness of this word of Mine: "My friend, wherefore art thou come hither?"

And, understanding it, would he not have felt that I still loved him, and that I sought his soul, that I might raise it up in pardoning his fault?

The traitor closed against himself the gate of

pardon, because he would not know Me in those revelations of My love, which I had made unto him.

My son, there are souls to which thou wilt speak of Me, and thy word shall remain for them a mystery, and those souls shall likewise shut against themselves the ways of mercy.

Then, I say unto thee, be thou sad, yet maintain thy peace, forasmuch as thou shalt have offered pardon to him who would not accept it.

And now, that I have said unto thee, "Be thou sad," I shall again say, "Be thou joyful;" for all do not thus shut their eyes to the light.

Because thine eyes have rested on the perfidious disciple, thou hast dreaded that thou couldst not prepare souls for pardon in revealing My tenderness to them.

Now, consider the man whom I shall show unto thee, and thou shalt know that he who knows Me has already entered into the holy ways of confidence and of sorrow.

When the hour was come when I was to accomplish My sacrifice, they who had condemned Me, led Me to that place called Calvary.

And when I reached that spot, I was nailed to a cross, and raised from the earth, for even as Moses elevated the brazen serpent in the desert, so likewise it was expedient that the Son of Man should be elevated, that He might attract all things unto Him.

And there were also two malefactors crucified,

and one of them blasphemed against Me, saying: "If Thou be Christ, save Thyself and us."

But the other, answering, rebuked him, saying: "Neither dost thou fear God, seeing that thou art under the same condemnation.

"And we indeed justly; for we receive the due reward of our deeds: but this Man hath done no evil."

And he said to Me: "Lord, remember me when Thou shalt come into Thy kingdom."

And I said to him: "Amen, I say to thee, this day thou shalt be with Me in Paradise."

And now, did not the end of this guilty man confirm My doctrine within thy mind?

Didst thou not see with thine eyes the wonders produced in his soul by the mere knowledge he had acquired concerning the Son of Man?

That criminal had been condemned by the justice of this world, and the hour was nigh when the justice of My Father was to convince him of sin.

But, lo! how the light from on high penetrates him, and that veil which had concealed Me from his eyes is riven asunder, and he recognizes Me.

He recognizes Me, for already he reprimands the blasphemer, he endeavours to confound him in taking My defence.

He knows Me, inasmuch as he protests against the punishment to which I am condemned; and, without fear, he confesses aloud that I have done no evil.

And, behold the prodigy suddenly operated

within him through this knowledge of the Son of Man.

Because he has known Me, he would not justify himself in My presence, but humbled himself in saying: "On our part it is merited, inasmuch as we only pay the penalty of our crimes."

And, as knowing Me, he was sensible that there was no crime on the earth which My heart does not pardon, in its love.

And knowing this, he hoped for the recompence of his repentance.

"Lord," he said unto Me, "remember me when Thou shalt be in Thy kingdom."

O My son, do thou preserve within thy heart the reply I made to that just man, and it will teach thee that I shed down pardon on human souls more promptly than the clouds of heaven pour down their salutary showers on a parched and arid ground.

Preserve likewise in mind the recollection of this man, on whom My Father bestowed understanding with the knowledge of My tenderness.

For this recollection will warn thee that many of thy brothers await from thee a revelation of My heart, that they may arrive by love and by confidence at that pardon which shall save them.

VII.

The Disciple.—O Master! I have learned from Thee, that in order to establish harmony amongst souls, it was expedient to love, and that he who loves, cries not aloud, nor does he make exception of persons, neither does he crush the bruised reed or extinguish the smoking torch.

I have learned from Thee to give utterance to words of sweetness and of mercy, and to come forth from the place of my repose, to seek those souls which do not come to me.

I have learned from Thee that the spirit is willing, and that the flesh is weak, and that he who loves pardons seventy times seven times, because pardon is the salvation of our erring brethren.

And now, Master, behold how fear has penetrated my bones, behold how the thoughts of my mind have been confounded.

I have been troubled, for I have seen Thy look inflamed, and Thy countenance become as that of an angry man.

Thy voice was moved, and its tones were, as it were, in contradiction with those lessons Thou didst impart unto me, inasmuch as I heard the sounds of terrible anathemas.

Thou didst speak, and Thou didst say:

"Woe unto you, Scribes and Pharisees, hypocrites, because you shut the gates of the kingdom of heaven against men. For you yourselves do not enter in, and those that are going in you suffer not to enter."

Thou didst say:

"Woe to you, Scribes and Pharisees, hypocrites, because you go round about the sea and the land to make one proselyte; and when he is made, you make him the child of hell twofold more than yourselves."

Thou didst say:

"Woe to you, blind guides, that say: Whosoever shall swear by the temple, it is nothing; but he that shall swear by the gold of the temple, is a debtor.

"And whosoever shall swear by the altar, it is nothing; but whosoever shall swear by the gift that is upon the altar, is a debtor.

"Ye blind guides: for whether is greater, the gift, or the altar that sanctifieth the gift?

"He, therefore, that sweareth by the altar, sweareth by it, and by all things that are upon it.

"And whosoever shall swear by the temple, sweareth by it, and by Him that dwelleth in it.

"And he that sweareth by heaven, sweareth by the throne of God, and by Him that sitteth thereon."

Thou didst say: "Woe to you, Scribes and Pharisees, hypocrites, because you tithe mint, and anise, and cummin, and have left the weightier things of the law, judgment, and mercy, and faith. These things you ought to have done, and not to leave those others undone.

"Blind guides, who strain at a gnat and swallow a camel."

And Thou didst say:

"Woe to you, Scribes and Pharisees, hypocrites, because you make clean the outside of the cup and of the dish, but within you are full of rapine and uncleanness.

"Thou blind Pharisee, first make clean the inside of the cup and of the dish, that the outside may become clean.

"Woe to you, Scribes and Pharisees, hypocrites, because you are like to whited sepulchres, which outwardly appear to men beautiful, but within are full of dead men's bones and of all filthiness:

"So you also outwardly indeed appear to men just, but inwardly you are full of hypocrisy and iniquity.

"Woe to you, Scribes and Pharisees, hypocrites, that build the sepulchres of the prophets and adorn the monuments of the just;

"And say: If we had been in the days of our fathers, we would not have been partakers with them in the blood of the prophets.

"Wherefore, you are witnesses against yourselves, that you are the sons of them that killed the prophets.

"Fill ye up the measure of your fathers.

"You serpents, generation of vipers, how will you flee from the judgment of hell?"

And now, O Master! that Thou hast spoken with vehemence, by what means shall I guard sweetness and love within my heart?

Is then Thy doctrine as that of men, a doctrine which varies and changes?

Do Thou expound to me these contradictions I have witnessed, and tell me if love can imprecate and condemn?

The Master.—My son, do thou beware of thus judging the severity of My words, and regarding them as though they were in contradiction with My doctrine.

Before being severe I was merciful, and My severity was but a supreme effort of love.

Before I raised My voice against the Scribes and Pharisees, how many times did I not pursue in their regard the ways of patience and meekness?

Didst thou not see Me enter the house of Simon, and accept his invitation to eat at his table?

And when I received the sinner who came to water My feet with her tears, didst thou not hear Me respond with meekness to the sentiment of indignation he conceived against Me?

And in order to enlighten his spirit, I speak of a certain creditor, who remits five pence to one debtor, and fifty to another.

And with that, I say to him: "Simon, which of these two debtors will love him the more?"

With a view to correct his pride, I show to him that the sinner had done more for Me than he himself.

Yet, in all these words, how much was there of meekness!

One day, the Pharisees, as seeking an occasion to tempt Me, led to Me a woman taken in adultery.

"Master," they said unto Me, "Moses in the law commanded us to stone such a one, what sayest Thou?"

And they said so, that they might accuse Me of prevarication, if I would claim a mitigation of the law, else of contradiction with Myself, if I would abandon her into their hands.

And didst thou not see Me remain silent; and My silence, was it not meant to instruct them without confounding them?

They pursued Me with their interrogations; they would have Me speak a word, and the word that I spoke was one meant to convince them of sin; but this word I uttered without harshness or bitterness.

Yet, another day, I said to the Scribes and Pharisees: "Which of you shall convince Me of sin? If I say the truth to you, why do you not believe Me?

"He that is of God, heareth the words of God. Therefore, you hear them not, because you are not of God."

The Jews, therefore, answered and said to Me: "Do we not say well that Thou art a Samaritan, and hast a devil?"

I answered: "I have not a devil, but I honour My Father, and you have dishonoured Me.

"But I seek not My own glory: there is one that seeketh and judgeth.

"Amen, amen, I say to you, if any man keep My word, he shall not see death for ever."

The Jews, therefore, said: "Now acknowledge that Thou hast a devil. Abraham is dead, and the prophets, and Thou sayest: If any man keep My word, he shall not taste death for ever.

"Art thou greater than our father Abraham, who is dead? And the prophets are dead. Whom dost Thou make Thyself?"

I answered: "If I glorify Myself, My glory is nothing. It is My Father that glorifieth Me, of whom you say that He is your God.

"And you have not known Him, but I know Him.

"And if I shall say that I know Him not, I shall be like to you, a liar. But I do know Him, and do keep His word.

"Abraham your father rejoiced that he might see My day; he saw it, and was glad."

The Jews then said to Me: "Thou art not yet fifty years old, and hast Thou seen Abraham?"

I said to them: "Amen, amen, I say to you, before Abraham was made, I Am."

They took up stones, therefore, to cast at Me. But I hid Myself, and went out of the temple.

Behold the injury done Me by the Jews; in their anger they seek an odious denunciation, and they find it in that word which they say unto Me: "Thou art a Samaritan."

I am silent, and make no reply to this first accusation.

Not being as yet satisfied, in their incensate

rage they invent a horrible blasphemy. "Thou art," they said, "one possessed by the devil."

I rebuke them without pronouncing an anathema, but in these simple terms: "I am not possessed by a devil; I seek the glory of My Father, and not My own."

They are once more irritated at this word of Mine; they know not what to reply: upon which they take up stones to cast at Me.

And, behold how, so as not to exercise My justice in striking them in their evil action, I hide Myself, and leave the temple.

Before showing severity towards the doctors of the law, the Scribes and the Pharisees, I pursued the ways of patience and meekness.

And now, if I abandoned these ways, do thou judge Me not, inasmuch as the hour is come when I shall reveal to thee why the look of the Son of Man was inflamed, and why His divine voice was moved.

May My grace be with thee, and thou shalt know that in the anathema I have comprised a mystery of love.

VIII.

The Master.—My son, true charity seeks to effect[1] good through means of meekness, but it likewise operates through force.

Be thou not astonished, then, if the word of the meekest of men has become like unto a hammer that breaks the stone, or like an impetuous wind that uproots the cedars.

When men understand not the voice of the heart, is it not expedient to carry out the work of their transformation by severity of language?

The Scribes and the Pharisees had heard that voice, and they remained insensible.

Was it not, then, better to disturb them in their works of iniquity by just menaces, than to abandon them to their reprobate sense?

For, does not true charity seek to bring back, through means of fear, those who will not be saved through those of love?

The Doctors of the law were charged to study the Scriptures, and they read the Scriptures, but they endeavoured not to comprehend them.

They had taken the key of science, and they had not entered its portals, inasmuch as they would not see in Me the promised Deliverer and the desired of nations.

They were charged to explain to the people the doctrine contained in the sacred book, and they deceived the people by a perverse doctrine;

Inasmuch as they hindered them from recognising Me as the Christ, the Son of the Living God.

They should have guided the people in the paths of justice, and they hid from their eyes that which was evil.

Forasmuch as they said: " Whosoever swears by the altar, is not bound; but he who swears by the offering on the altar, is a debtor."

After having, during a certain time, held Myself in patience and meekness towards those blind guides, should I not, for the salvation of the people, lower them in the esteem of the people?

And, moreover, He who came to re-establish all things by the virtue of His love, should He not likewise unmask the wolf when he appeared in the garment of the shepherd ?

The Scribes and Pharisees believed themselves justified, and by My meekness I could not succeed in convincing them of iniquity, forasmuch as their eyes were not opened to the foulness of their hands.

They devoured the substance of the widows, they paid the tithes of the mint, of the anise, and of the cummin, but, they abandoned the most essential part of the law, which is justice and fidelity.

They practised exteriorly the works which justify in the eyes of men, whilst they were internally all corruption and rapine.

Was it not expedient to humble them in their pride, with a view to undeceive them ?

Thou hast read that which is written: "Happy is he whom God chastises Himself: reject not the chastisement of the Most High." Inasmuch as when He speaks, He bestows the remedy; and if His hand wounds, it likewise heals.

You have heard the words of the prophet: "I sinned before I was humbled; it is good, O Lord, that Thou shouldst have humbled me, that I may learn Thy ordinances, which are full of justice."

And now, how should I have humbled the Scribes and Pharisees, had I not removed with violence the bandage which hindered them from seeing the malice of their thoughts and of their actions?

And how should I have humbled them, had I not searched into their hearts, with a view to exhibit in open day the abominations of their lives?

The Scribes and Pharisees believed themselves just, and, in so believing themselves, they were hardened and pitiless.

When sinners approached them, they fled, as though they might contract some stain by their presence.

In the assemblies they would have no manner of communication with them, and they imagined they did rightly in repulsing them with harshness.

Like unto birds of prey, they were not to be seen beside sinners, but at those hours when they could submit them to the rigour of the law.

When they prayed in the temple, their prayer

was not accompanied by the confession of their misery.

They opened their mouths but to extol themselves, and not to sound the praises of God; and in lauding themselves, they feared not to speak with contempt of the publicans, whom they called sinners.

"O God," they said, "we give Thee thanks that we are not as the rest of men, extortioners, unjust, adulterers, as are likewise these publicans."

And as these proud men thus repulsed the guilty, did they not merit to be treated themselves as they had acted by others?

They knew I was the friend of sinners, inasmuch as they made a crime of My receiving them with charity, and seeking them with love.

They knew this, and they had heard Me answer their accusations in these words: "The Son of Man is not come to lose men, but to save them."

And, as the knowledge of these things had not moved them, and had not given them entrails of mercy, was it not expedient to make them taste the bitterness of reproach, so as to create a new spirit within them?

The husbandman gently upraises on its stalk the ear of corn that he finds bent to the earth, for he knows that the ear will not resist in his hand.

But, so does he not with the great tree bent by the storm; as, knowing that his hand is insufficient, he employs an instrument of wood or of iron, and thus straightens it with force.

And it is after this manner that the Son of Man would raise up by meekness those who were meek, and by rigour the harsh and the pitiless.

The Disciple.—The Scribes and Pharisees are dead, and I have rejoiced, because I shall not assume an austere mien, or shall not raise my voice beyond measure.

I have rejoiced, inasmuch as I shall work to create harmony among souls, without abandoning the ways of meekness.

The Master.—In truth, the Scribes and Pharisees are dead, and yet, I say unto you, they are still in the midst of you, forasmuch as their race is not extinct.

Many infuse into men's minds the venom of false doctrine, and sow in all places both error and falsehood.

And, those seduce their brothers, because they use My words with malice, and interpret them according to the perverse desires of their hearts.

Many resemble whitened sepulchres, whose exterior seems fair in the eyes of men, but which are filled with the bones of the dead, and with all filthiness.

And those believe themselves just, because they appear so before men; and supposing themselves just, they treat their brothers with harshness.

Now, I say unto thee, even as I did not spare

the Pharisees, neither do thou spare those who resemble them.

What, then, would be thy love if thou didst leave to perish many amongst thy brethren, so as not to chagrin some few amongst them?

He who is guilty of homicide, is deserving of death, and he who kills the soul, shall he not merit to be chastised by words of severity?

Is it not just that the hypocrites, on whose heads one day shall fall the blood of the people, forasmuch as they shall have led them to their ruin, is it not just that they should be humbled themselves, in presence of the people, in witnessing the public condemnation of their doctrine?

I say to thee once more, even as I raised My voice against the Scribes and the Pharisees, by reason of their harshness towards sinners, even so do thou condemn those men who resemble them.

Those also are pitiless, and by their harshness they close the ways of pardon against their brothers, in destroying within them confidence, with love and repentance.

If thou wilt not treat them as they treat other men, the day will come when compassion can no more enter their hearts.

Therefore, do thou enforce with the scourge the spirit of mercy, in treating with those who are themselves without mercy.

For, I say to thee in truth, these are more guilty than were the buyers and sellers who had made of the house of My Father a den of thieves.

The Disciple.—O Master! I have thrilled with

anguish; do Thou tell me that which Thou seest.

The Master.—I see men rise up and draw close to each other, like unto the black and dense vapours that precede the tempest.

I see these men turn pale with rage and fury; they have spoken, and they have said: "Woe to him who shall reveal our hypocrisy; woe to him who shall not be hard and pitiless as we ourselves."

The Disciple.—O Master! what further dost Thou see?

The Master.—My son, fear thou not, I have seen Satan re-descend to the depths of the abyss, and I have seen thy heart triumph by the force of its love.

THE VISION.

THE VISION.

The Disciple.—And as I had heard these last words of My Divine Master, behold how I was transported in spirit to the summit of a very high mountain, and at the foot of the mountain there was a great valley.

And the angel who had transported me thither opened my eyes.

And, I beheld a vast multitude of men who came from all sides, inasmuch as the great valley was open to the east and to the west, to the north and to the south.

And I beheld prodigious phenomena in the sun, in the moon, in the stars, and on the face of the earth.

The nations were in consternation at the trouble occasioned by the roaring of the sea, and of the waves, and men withered with fear at the expectation of that which was to come.

The sun grew dim, the moon refused her light, the stars fell from the heavens, and the powers of heaven were shaken.

Then, I beheld the sign of the Son of Man appear in the heavens, and all tribes of the earth mourned.

And, they beheld the Son of Man coming in the clouds of heaven with much power and majesty.

And at the same time the Son of Man sent His angels with a trumpet and with a great voice, and they assembled all men from the four corners of the earth.

And when the Son of Man was come in the splendour of His majesty, and all the angels with Him, He seated Himself on the seat of His Majesty.

All the nations were gathered together before Him, and He separated them into two bands, as the shepherd separates the sheep from the goats, and He set one on His right hand and the other on His left.

And when the great separation was made, an angel passed near me, and my ears were opened, and I heard the Son of Man say to those who were on His right hand:

"Come, ye blessed of My Father, possess the kingdom prepared for you from the foundation of the world; for, I was hungry, and you gave Me to eat; I was thirsty, and you gave Me to drink; I was a stranger, and you took Me in; naked, and you clothed Me; sick, and you visited Me; I was in prison, and you came to Me."

Thereupon, I heard the just answer Him: "Lord, when did we see Thee hungry, and fed Thee; thirsty, and gave Thee to drink? and when did we see Thee a stranger, and took Thee in; or naked, and clothed Thee; or when did we see Thee sick, or in prison, and came to Thee?"

And the Son of Man answered them: "Amen, I say to you, as long as you did it to one of these My least brethren, you did it to Me."

And the judgment being ended, an angel passed by, and my ears were opened a second time, and I heard the Son of Man say to those who were on His left:

"Depart from Me, ye cursed, into eternal fire, which was prepared for the devil and his angels.

"For I was hungry, and you gave Me not to eat; I was thirsty, and you gave Me not to drink; I was a stranger, and you took Me not in; naked, and you clothed Me not; sick, and in prison, and you did not visit Me."

And I heard those who were placed on the left hand of the Son of Man exclaim, in their turn:

"Lord, when did we see Thee hungry and thirsty, or a stranger, or naked, or sick, or in prison, and we did not minister to Thee?"

And the Son of Man answered them: "Amen, I say to you, as long as you did it not to one of these least ones, you did it not to Me."

And, behold, how, after having heard this judgment, I was troubled in the powers of my soul, and, seized with an ineffable anguish, I exclaimed:

"Lord, Lord, these Thy judgments, are they just and equitable?

"Thou hast said: Children of men, you shall adore the Lord your God, and Him alone you shall serve."

And I beheld amongst those whom Thou didst

place at Thy right, men who have not always practised this word of Thy mouth.

And they have suffered themselves to be distracted by present and flitting goods, and it is at the close of their career alone, that, remembering Thy law, they have adored in spirit and in truth.

They commenced by serving the great and the powerful of the earth, and all those from whom they hoped for gold and for glory, and they awaited the hour when all force abandons each living creature, to serve the Master of all things.

They gave unto Him from whom they derived life and intelligence, they gave unto Him but the wreck of mind and of heart.

Lord, Lord, are Thy judgments just and equitable?

And Thou hast said: "O children of men! My house shall be styled the house of prayer; and I say unto you in truth, this place is terrible, inasmuch as it is the gate of heaven."

And I see amongst those whom Thou hast placed at Thy right hand, men who profaned Thy holy temple.

They entered its sanctuary, they humbled their heads beneath its dome, they bent their knees, but their hearts were without words, without life.

Their looks blessed Thee not, because they suffered the thoughts of their minds to wander afar, in forming vain projects within them.

Their lips praised Thee not, because their hearts, abandoned to evil desires, took delight in guilty emotions.

And, behold, how they go forth from the house of prayer, as from the tabernacles of the impious, because they had placed stumbling-blocks in the place where Thy name should be invoked.

Lord, Lord, are Thy judgments just and equitable?

Thou didst say: "He who exalts himself shall be humbled, and he who humbles himself shall be exalted, inasmuch as I resist the proud, and I give My grace to the humble."

And I see amongst those whom Thou hast placed at Thy right hand, men who opened their hearts to the inordinate love of glory and power.

They raised themselves above their brothers by the means of injustice, they subjected them to their empire in making them serve as a footstool.

Thou didst smite them in their madness, and, as not knowing why Thy hand had smitten them, they rebelled against the designs of heaven.

Their lips were sullied with murmurs, whose echoes resounded afar, and they caused the angels of peace to weep at their blasphemies.

In their insatiable thirst, they contemned both repose, and honour, and life, so eager were they of enjoyment.

They expended all the work of their hands in acquiring that which was to be their ruin; they sought death with avidity, by the errors of their lives, and they allied themselves with it.

Lord, Lord, are Thy judgments just and equitable?

The Master.—My son, I have said, blessed are the merciful, because they shall obtain mercy; and, behold wherefore My judgments are both just and equitable.

Truly, truly, several of those whom I have placed on My right hand, contemned My law, and had sullied their hands, but, behold how My eye had discovered some works of love in the midst of their iniquities.

And, forasmuch as My eye had discerned these works, I came down to them at the last hour.

I displayed to their eyes the truth which enlightens, and they broke the idols of their worship, and they worshipped that which they had once despised.

Their hearts were moved in presence of My tenderness, even as the child is moved by the mother's tears, and they tended unto Me as to their source, in sorrow and in confidence.

And, behold, why I have said to those who had not always followed the ways of rectitude: "Come, ye blessed of My Father, take possession of the kingdom which was prepared for you from the foundation of the world."

And now, if I reward by grace, and by mercy, and by glory, him in whom I discover some works of love, shall I not inebriate from the abundance of My mansion him who shall have loved with plenitude in Me and through Me?

O thou who lovest souls, forasmuch as thou didst love Me first, remember My judgments, await with patience, the hour is nigh when thou shalt receive the true joy.

The Disciple.—Behold how, after having heard these words of the Master, I was once more seized with unutterable anguish, and I exclaimed:

"Lord, Lord, are Thy judgments just and equitable?"

Thou hast said: "Blessed are the poor in spirit, for theirs is the kingdom of heaven; blessed are they who mourn, for they shall be comforted."

And I see amongst those whom Thou hast placed on Thy left, men who had not desired the riches that perish.

They had endured, without murmuring, hunger and thirst, and nakedness, because they were mindful that, whilst the foxes have their dens, the Son of Man had not a stone whereon to pillow His head.

Lord, Lord, are Thy judgments just and equitable?

Thou hast said: "Blessed are they who hunger and thirst after justice, for they shall be filled."

And I see amongst those on my left, men whose hearts had been consumed by the love of all justice.

They were husbands, and they disowned their guilty partners, with a view to prove unto all men that they condemned all adultery.

They were fathers, and they cursed their

children, that they might prove to all men that they condemned all revolt and impiety.

They were brothers, and they abandoned their sisters in their ignominy, so as to prove unto all that they held all stains of vice in abhorrence.

Lord, Lord, are Thy judgments just and equitable?

The Master.—My son, I have said, judgment without mercy is reserved for him who has not shown mercy, and behold why My judgments are just and equitable.

Truly, truly, several of those whom I have placed on My left had detached their hearts from perishable riches, they had condemned all adultery, all revolt, and all contamination.

Yet, behold how My eyes have discovered within them both harshness and disdain.

They wounded by the malignant word those who followed not the ways of rectitude, and consequently, those have closed their ears to the words of life.

They pardoned a first and a second time, their fallen brother, but they did not pardon seventy times seven times, and their brother was not raised from his abjection by confidence, by love, or by pardon.

And, because My eyes have discovered that in the midst of their works of justice they had not shown mercy, I have abandoned them at their last hour to the power of the spirits of darkness, who are the angels of harshness and hatred.

And, behold, wherefore I have said to those who

had groaned and lamented, and whose hearts had seemed perfect in the eyes of men :

"Depart from Me, ye cursed, into eternal fire, prepared for the devil and his angels."

O thou who lovest souls, because thou didst love Me first, remember My judgments, wait in patience, the hour is nigh when thou shalt receive the true joy.

The Disciple.—O Master! I return Thee thanks, because Thou hast enlightened my eyes, and because Thou hast directed me in Thy ways.

Lord! Lord! Thou art great in all Thy works, and Thy judgments are just and equitable.

Behold how, in unison with the Ancients prostrate before Thy throne, I exclaim :

"To Him who is seated on the throne, and to the Lamb, benediction, glory, honour, and power, throughout all ages of ages."

As I had finished these words, I was transported in spirit to the heights where shines forth the fulness of light, and I heard a voice proclaiming:

"Love for eternity."

THE END.

PRINTED BY RICHARDSON AND SON, DERBY.